KV-393-211

RECOLLECTIONS OF
AJAHN CHAH

Recollections of Ajahn Chah

For Free Distribution
Sabbadānaṃ dhammadānaṃ jināti
The gift of the Dhamma surpasses all other gifts.

Published by Amaravati Publications,
Amaravati Buddhist Monastery,
Hertfordshire, Great Britain
publications@amaravati.org
www.amaravati.org

Produced by Aruno Publications,
Aruna Ratanagiri Buddhist Monastery,
Northumberland, Great Britain
www.ratanagiri.org.uk

This book is available for free download at
www.forestsanghabooks.org

ISBN 978-1-870205-65-8

Copyright © 2013 AMARAVATI PUBLICATIONS

Cover design by Nicholas Halliday

If you are interested in translating this text into another language, contact us for formatting guidelines, text material, and help with copyright issues.

This work is licensed under a Creative Commons
Attribution-NonCommercial-NoDerivs 3.0 Unported Licence.
http://creativecommons.org/licenses/by-nc-nd/3.0/

See page 169 for more details on your rights and restrictions under this licence.

Produced with the L^AT_EX typesetting system. Typeset in Gentium font distributed by SIL International, and Crimson Text font created by Sebastian Kosch.

Second edition, 15,000 copies, 2013, Printed in Malaysia

We would like to acknowledge the support of
many people in the preparation of this book,
especially that of the Kataññutā group
in Malaysia, Singapore and Australia
for bringing it into production.

CONTENTS

Part I

INTERVIEWS WITH SENIOR SANGHA MEMBERS

1

BEING WITH AJAHN CHAH

The first chapter of this book has been adapted from a series of transcribed interviews which were conducted by Ajahn Kongrit Ratanawanno during his time at Amaravati Buddhist Monastery, UK. Ajahn Kongrit's home monastery is Wat Beung Saensook, Thailand. In most cases the interviewee was asked the simple question of what had inspired them most in being with Ajahn Chah.

Ajahn Sumedho

Luang Por Chah had a great deal of *mettā* (loving-kindness) and I felt welcomed by the way he received me at Wat Pah Pong – he seemed to be interested in me. I felt intuitively that this was a very wise man. At the time I couldn't understand Thai very well, but what I saw of how he lived his life and his general way of being was very pleasing to me. His teaching was very direct and he was able to see very quickly where I was at.

He didn't want me to spend time reading or studying, just to practise. He emphasized everybody's *paṭipat* (practice). When I first came to him, he told me to put my books away and to just read the *citta*, my mind. I was happy to do that, because I was weary of studying Buddhism and wanted to practise it instead of just reading about it. This was what he was encouraging me to do.

Though he gave a lot of talks, which I couldn't properly understand for the first two years, he emphasized *kor wat* (monastic duties), the way you live in the monastery: paying attention, being mindful with food and the robes, and with the *kuṭī* (hut) and the monastery. He was like a mirror that would reflect my state of mind. He always seemed to be completely present. I'd get carried away with thoughts and emotions sometimes, but by just being around him, I found that I could suddenly let go – I could drop what I was holding onto without even telling him. His presence helped me to see what I was doing and what I was attached to. So I decided that I would live with him as long as I could, since such monks are hard to find. I stayed with him for ten years at Wat Pah Pong and at various branch monasteries.

Ajahn Pasanno

I cannot say there is really any single thing that impressed me most, there were many things that impressed me. Certainly

Luang Por Chah set an example for us in the sense that he didn't just teach from theory; when he taught he was always present – he was an example of what was skilful and beautiful.

The images that come to mind are of Luang Por himself being a great teacher and everybody respecting him so much. But I also remember a senior monk coming to visit Wat Pah Pong, and Luang Por paying respects to and looking after this monk. Seeing the teaching in action without his 'being the Teacher' really impressed me. It was a very direct teaching on not-self and a living example of the ease and freedom that come from penetrating not-self: neither a theory, nor a Buddhist philosophy. That was the way he taught us: living the example, rather than just giving us the philosophy. He had a great ability to teach and draw people to the Dhamma by using these ordinary life situations.

I remember one time we were coming back from *piṇḍapat* (alms-round) and I was walking along behind him. My Thai was not so good, so I was just being respectful and walking close by him. We came in from the back of the monastery, and as we were walking through the forest, two lizards fell from a tree. Luang Por looked, then turned and said, 'See those lizards, they were mating. If they weren't caught in sensuality they wouldn't have fallen and hurt themselves like this!' It was very simple, and for a new monk a very funny and direct teaching.

These are very real situations, very ordinary, and very to the point. Luang Por's ability to give examples and point to the things around us empowered us to see Dhamma ourselves, rather than looking to scripture or looking to him. To see that Dhamma is all around us and is something we can see for ourselves was very empowering. It was both direct and had that human quality.

This 'humanness' of Luang Por Chah was really quite striking. One time he had some skin problems and I was helping him put ointment on the inflammation. I would have to take off his *sabong* (under-robe) to spread the ointment all around his bottom, back and legs. And he asked, 'Look at my bottom, does it look beautiful?' Then he would say, 'It is not beautiful, nobody would want it like this! Everybody who gets old, they all look like this.' Again, this is taking the ordinary and making it something that allows us to relinquish, to let go.

There was also his extraordinary generosity: his willingness to give of himself, to give to people, his compassion. That was always very touching. He never really put himself first. There was one year I was living at Wat Pah Pong and acting as his attendant. I had been a monk for many years by then and my Thai was very good, so I could understand his teaching and what he was doing. I used to stay with him until night-time, and put him to bed and massage him. It would be very rare for him to go to bed before midnight, and sometimes he would be up until 1 or 2 a.m. Yet he was always willing to help people who were interested in Dhamma; to give, to teach, to train, and never thought about keeping anything for himself – complete relinquishment, complete renunciation. It was very powerful.

But it was very difficult to be his *upatthak* (attendant)! It was really hard work because he never had a schedule, just responding to situations in an appropriate way. His flexibility came from generosity and compassion, not from any logical sequence of how things should be. That was always very impressive. So there are many different aspects of living with Luang Por Chah. It's difficult to pin it down to just one. If you ask me the same question tomorrow, different things will come to mind.

Ajahn Ṭhiradhammo

The most meaningful and impressive aspect to me was that he was a living embodiment of the Buddha's teachings, which I had only previously read about and understood conceptually.

The first meaningful example was when I went to live at Wat Pah Pong. I thought that if I was living in the monasteries under his guidance, I should get to know who this great teacher Ajahn Chah was and what his basic teaching was. I arrived there a month before the Rains Retreat began, when there was a less formal schedule. Thus in the evening one of the best learning situations was to sit at Ajahn Chah's hut and listen to him interacting with visitors and resident monks. Since my Thai was passable I could understand most of what was said. However, as I listened to Ajahn Chah's advice, counsel and teachings, I began to feel more confused about who he was and what his teaching was. I noticed that he gave different teachings to different people, sometimes even giving contrary advice. To me he thus came across as being inconsistent. So what was it? Was he just putting on a front, or was he confused? This presented something of a spiritual dilemma for me. On the one hand Ajahn Chah was obviously an inspiring teacher, displaying considerable wisdom and charisma. On the other hand, his teachings were not consistent with how I thought an 'enlightened being' should be.

Then one evening as I listened to him, it suddenly occurred to me that there was *no fixed and consistent Ajahn Chah.* Rather than being a person with a particular teaching, he was actually just responding with mindfulness and wisdom to whatever situation arose. His apparent inconsistency was in effect a specific wise response to what the particular person or situation required at that time. I had previously been relating to Ajahn Chah as someone with a stable personality and a set body of beliefs and views. Now it dawned on me that he was not holding on to a fixed personality or definite views, but was the living expression of mindfulness and wisdom. What appeared to be inconsistency on the conventional level was in truth a relevant and immediate response to whatever was happening at the time. To me this was a living example of impersonality.

Another example which was exceptionally helpful to me personally was when I was bothered by the phenomenon of people's faces coming up in meditation. They were not usually frightening, but just bothersome and distracting. I wasn't sure what this meant or what caused it, and became preoccupied with trying to understand or do something with it. Fortunately I was able to ask Ajahn Chah about this. He called it 'mental phenomena' and said, 'Just observe it, and don't be fascinated by it. Know it and go back to the breathing.' He explained that we can become attracted by such things because they're new and interesting. He said that I might either become quite excited about them, thinking I had psychic powers like precognition, seeing the face of someone who next day might offer food, or I might think that maybe ghosts were haunting me. This was the best and most useful advice on the problem I had received from any teacher, and when I could apply it, the faces eventually faded away. And this principle has been very helpful for me in dealing with many of the unusual phenomena which arise in spiritual practice.

Ajahn Sucitto

The first time I saw Luang Por Chah was when he landed in Britain, when he came through the arrivals at Heathrow Airport. There was a group of us monks: Ajahn Sumedho, Ānando, Viradhammo, and myself. Ajahn Pabhākaro was with Luang Por Chah. The first thing that I noticed about him was that he was quite small, particularly compared with Ajahn Pabhākaro. But he looked like a very, very big man – he carried himself like a big man; not aggressive, but completely confident. He looked like he had a lot of space inside him.

Here he was in a foreign country, he'd come from a long plane journey, couldn't speak the language, but he looked completely in charge and he knew exactly where he wanted to be. He was not hurried. He was not anxious. He was balanced in himself and looked warm and friendly – not in charge in a hard way, but at ease within his environment. Whenever we came to see him, he was receptive; he knew how to receive people. He was like your favourite uncle, as if you'd just been talking to him and you'd known him all your life; very easy, very warm and you immediately felt very relaxed. Normally when you meet somebody who's strange, you think, 'Better make sure everything's all right...' But with him you felt relaxed because there was the presence of *mettā* – immediately. This was overwhelming in some ways because usually almost everybody takes a little bit of time before they warm up.

He stayed at the Hampstead Vihāra in London. This was just a small town house. Compared with the big space of Wat Pah Pong it had very narrow corridors and small rooms, and it was crowded. Yet he was comfortable there. He had women sitting quite close to him, but it was no problem. People were not doing things properly according to the Thai way of doing things – not deliberately, but just not doing things in the proper way. And I could sense that some of the monks were quite anxious to make sure it was all right, but he seemed to stay at ease.

When people asked him questions, of course he couldn't understand their words. So Ajahn Sumedho or Ajahn Pabhākaro would translate – but he kept his focus on the questioner. If somebody asked some very complicated question – about the Abhidhamma, for example – he would respond to the questioner rather than the question, saying things like, 'Thinking too much is not good for you', or, 'Sometimes it's like this and sometimes it's like that.' It was always a very simple answer that went deeper than the question. It went straight to the heart. He was never fooled by any of the questions; he always went straight to the heart. He could feel where people were coming from.

He was very kind: often humorous, but not dismissive. He never wavered from being receptive and patient. People would be affected by that. People could feel that immediate heart contact and the effect was amazing. Sometimes the place would be crowded with people who'd sit there just so they could be there. They didn't have any questions. They just wanted to be there, just to feel that heart contact. People are usually nervous, tense and anxious, so to be in a place where there was somebody like this, offering this ease and clarity, was a blessing. You couldn't understand what he was saying and you didn't have anything to ask, but still you wanted to be there. It would go on for hours. He never seemed to change his pace. He never hurried; he never hung back. Everything was just flowing. Never hurrying, never stopping, and never moving back. It was always flowing along, like still flowing water. That image is what he was like: still flowing water.

Ajahn Munindo

During the time I was with or nearby Luang Por Chah, I was aware he was making a powerful impression on me, but it was only many years later that I became clearer about just what it was that had been impressed upon me. At the time of living in Thailand it was perhaps more like an intuition of the 'rightness' of staying there, even though it was certainly not easy.

I heard that somebody once asked Luang Por Chah, 'How come, out of all the monks in Thailand, you stand out as different?' Luang Por replied, 'I was willing to be daring. Others wouldn't dare do as I did.' I didn't hear this exchange directly, it was reported to me later, but it had a significant effect on my own attitude to practice. It signalled where the priority lay. Knowing this about his attitude helped me to understand his teachings better.

Luang Por Chah wasn't worried about being popular or famous or rich, or having lots of disciples. If he felt that something was right and should be done, he would do it. Sometimes that took daring. From the stories of his experiences in practice it was clear that he had to dare to confront his own fears and resistances. He had to dare so as not to be intimidated by the things that normally limit others. He had to dare to contradict the views of others, even when they were strongly held.

During the five years I was near him, the thing that continually inspired me was how totally agile he was. My recollection of how he handled situations stays with me and serves as a valuable support in dealing with all that we have to face here in the West. I think I had some sense of the way he just flowed, without resistance. Whether it was important dignitaries coming to visit, or a simple villager who was concerned about a sick water buffalo, or rich supporters from Bangkok, he always had the same beautiful ability to 'go with it'. Sometimes he would be surrounded by a large gathering of monks hanging on his every word, and at other times he might just be sitting on his own with one or two young monks, chewing betel nut and drinking coca cola. He was always able to adjust without stress. There were none of the tell-tale signs of clinging which produce suffering in an individual and generate an atmosphere of artificiality. He was as natural as I could wish a human being to be. I don't think I have ever seen anyone so thoroughly normal. Luang Por was at home wherever he went, whatever he did. He could be quiet and sensitive when you went to see him about some personal struggle, and a few minutes later he would be shouting orders at the huge crowd of soldiers who had come to help build his new temple.

This teaching example identified for me how much resistance I still had, and that this struggling 'for' and 'against' life was the source of the problem. Sometimes we think our difficulties are caused by external circumstances, but usually the biggest cause is our inner habits of clinging. Luang Por didn't show any signs of resistance and accordingly didn't manifest suffering. This state of non-suffering was real for him, and it was remarkable how evident it also was outwardly. Because he had settled the great questions in his own heart, he was a catalyst for harmony and well-being in the outer world. To have had the good fortune to witness that was a blessing.

Ajahn Amaro

One of the most impressive things about Luang Por Chah was the way that he could display authority without being authoritarian. He was a very good leader but not someone who had to dominate people. I didn't live with him for a long time, and maybe the very first time I had an exchange with him was in about April or May 1978, when I was an *anāgārika* (postulant) and Luang Por was staying with us at Wat Pah Nanachat. As an *anāgārika* I was the attendant to Ajahn Pabhākaro, who was the abbot of the monastery. So it was my job to get his robes and bowl ready for *piṇḍapat* in the morning. I never found it easy to get up early in the morning; I still don't. Morning is not my best time – I can do it as an act of will, but I have to make the effort.

On this particular morning I woke up and saw light coming through the gaps between the planks of the walls. I thought, 'Wow, the moon is really bright tonight.' Then I looked at the clock and saw that it must have stopped, and I realized, 'That's not the moon; that's the sun.' So I leapt up, threw my clothes on and raced down the path. When I got to the back of the *sāla* (main hall), all the other people had already gone out for *piṇḍapāt*, but Ajahn Pabhākaro and Luang Por, who were going out on a nearby *piṇḍapāt*, still hadn't left. I thought, 'OK, I've still got time. Maybe they didn't notice.' I then realized it was twenty-five past and they were going to leave at half-past. So I got their robes, hoping they hadn't noticed I'd arrived late and had missed the morning chanting and sitting. While I was down by Ajahn Chah's feet tying up the bottom end of his robes, he said something in Thai which I couldn't understand. I looked up slightly anxiously at Ajahn Pabhākaro for translation. Ajahn Chah had a big grin on his face, an incredibly friendly, loving smile. Then Ajahn Pabhākaro translated, 'Sleep is delicious.' That was the first time in my life when I did something wrong, but instead of being criticized or punished was met by an extraordinarily loving attitude. It was at that point that something in my heart knew Buddhism was really very different from anything I had encountered previously.

Luang Por was also very flexible. He had no respect for time. And he didn't have any respect for logical consistency. He could change his mind or his approach in a finger-snap. A couple of years later, when Ajahn Sumedho was starting up Chithurst monastery, I was thinking of going back to England to visit my family. I got a telegram saying my father was very ill with a heart attack, so I came down from Roi-Et and then to Wat Pah Pong to pay respects to Luang Por and ask his advice. I felt I should leave for England soon, but my question was how I should go about this. My Thai was pretty poor, and on that occasion Ajahn Jāgaro was translating. I explained to Luang Por that I only had one Rains Retreat as a monk and that I was from England; my family lived quite near Chithurst and my father had just had a heart attack and was very sick, and what did Luang Por think I should do?

He spoke for about twenty minutes – it was a long speech and I didn't really catch much of it. At the end, Ajahn Jāgaro said, 'Well, he said four things.

' "Go to England and when your visit to your family is finished, go and pay your respects to Ajahn Sumedho and then come straight back to Thailand.

' "Go to England and stay with your family and when your business with your family is finished, go to stay with Ajahn Sumedho for a year and then after that year you should come back to Thailand.

' "Go to England, stay with your family, when your business with your family is finished, go stay with Ajahn Sumedho and help him out. If it gets too difficult, you can come back to Thailand if you really want to.

' "Go to England, when the business with the family is finished, go and stay with Ajahn Sumedho and don't come back." '

The whole talk was delivered with exactly the same expression. It wasn't as if any one option was preferable. As he was speaking, each single option was an absolutely sincere piece of advice, a directive: 'Do this. These are your instructions. Follow them to the letter!' And he wasn't trying to be clever. It was obvious that he was being absolutely straightforward.

Related to that was his quality of being transparent as a person. Someone once asked me to take a message to him, saying that some people had just arrived at the *sāla* and could he come to meet them. So I went to his *kuṭī*, where he was sitting on his rattan bench with his eyes closed. There was no one else around. I went up and knelt in front of him and he didn't open his eyes. So I waited a few minutes, wondering what to do, but he still didn't open his eyes. So I said (in Thai), 'Excuse me, Luang Por' and he opened his eyes. But it was as if there was absolutely nobody there. He wasn't asleep; his eyes opened, but there was no expression on his face. It was completely empty. He looked at me, and I looked at him and said, 'Luang Por, Ajahn Chu asked me to bring a message that some people have come to the *sāla* and would it be possible for you to come and receive them?'

Again for a moment there was no expression, just this completely spacious, empty quality on his face. Then out of nowhere, the personality appeared. He made some remark that I didn't quite catch and it was as if suddenly the 'person' appeared; it was like watching a being coming into existence.

There was an extraordinary quality in that moment, seeing a being putting on a mask or a costume, as if to say, 'OK, I'll be Ajahn Chah. I can play at being Ajahn Chah for these people.' You could see that assumption of the personality, the body, all the characteristics of personhood just being taken up as if he was putting on his robe or taking up a role for the sake of emerging and contacting other people. It was very powerful, seeing that 'something' coming out of nothing; seeing a being appearing before your eyes.

Ajahn Jayasāro

I arrived at Wat Pah Pong in December 1978. It was the *uposatha* (observance) day. I was already an *anāgārika* but I hadn't shaved my head. I had been travelling. One of the Western monks, Tan Pamutto, took me to his *kuṭī* and shaved my head, and then we went to pay respects to Luang Por. The moment I saw him I had a very strong feeling that he would be my teacher, and that I didn't need to go anywhere else.

Before I left England, Ajahn Sumedho gave me a piece of advice. He said, 'Don't look for the perfect monastery, it doesn't exist.' Even so I got a little side-tracked and went to stay with another teacher for a few days. But then I came back to Wat Pah Pong and thought, 'Now I can stop travelling.'

I felt Luang Por was unlike anybody I had ever met before. I felt he was the only totally normal person I had ever met – everyone else was a bit abnormal compared to him! It felt as if I'd spent my whole life listening to people singing just a little bit out of tune, and this was the first time I'd ever heard someone sing in tune. Or as if I'd grown up in a country that only had plastic flowers, and then one day I finally saw a real flower: 'Ah, so that's what a real flower is. I've only ever seen plastic flowers before.' Plastic flowers can be beautiful, but they're nothing like real flowers.

Question: Ajahn Chah couldn't speak English, and you, when you came, couldn't speak Thai, so how did you learn from him?

Answer: The teaching that you receive in a *desanā* (Dhamma talk) and in other verbal teachings is only one part of what you get from a teacher. From the very first day, the thing that I received from Ajahn Chah, and the thing that impressed me most, was this very strong confidence that he was an enlightened being, and therefore that enlightenment is real and possible. I had that belief before from books I'd read, and to a certain extent from other teachers, but it was only when I met Ajahn Chah that this became really grounded in my being, this confidence that the path to Nibbāna can still be followed and that it is possible to realize all the fruits of the Holy Life. So I was impressed by who Ajahn Chah was, his being, as much as by his teaching. Of course I was very inspired by his teachings, and there are many teachings that I treasure and have made great use of in my practice.

When you become a monk, you go through periods of feeling very positive, and you can also go through periods when you feel discouraged and very unhappy. I think if you look closely at what sustains you when you feel down, it's not so much the wise teachings and reflections as the faith that what you're doing is really meaningful, and that the path of practice does lead to Nibbāna. I've never had any disrobing doubts since I became a monk. Other monks who understood or studied the teachings more than I have disrobed. It didn't help them. But because I had the presence of Ajahn Chah and afterwards the memory of Ajahn Chah, it seemed to me there's no alternative, there's nothing else that makes sense except to be a monk and to follow this path.

I also loved his being and how he expressed himself, his voice. If you gave Ajahn Chah a newspaper to read out loud, or if he were just to read names from a telephone directory, I could still listen to him for hours.

Ajahn Khemanando

Most of my own personal experience of Ajahn Chah comes from the period, beginning in January 1979, when I came to stay at Wat Pah Pong as a layman, followed by many months as an *anāgārika* or *pa-khao* (postulant). I was a newcomer to Thailand and monastic life, and spoke or understood very little Thai, being quite dependent on the more senior Western monks for translations and explanations of what was happening. So my impressions from that time were not so much of profound dialogues or specific instructions on meditation, but more revelations of Ajahn Chah's character, which would often overturn my own pre-conceptions about the nature of an enlightened being, whilst also, sometimes simultaneously, providing evidence that he did indeed function on quite a different level from the people by whom he was surrounded; apparently small incidents in which Ajahn Chah would do things that didn't need explaining, which I was able to observe to gain some food for thought.

Once I and a fellow *pa-khao*, a New Zealander, were whiling away a hot, steamy afternoon in idle conversation on the balcony of my *kuṭī*. At Wat Pah Pong in those days, much of the formal practice was done as a group activity in the main hall morning and evening, while your individual *kuṭī* was kind of sacrosanct, where you could expect to be left to your own devices most of the time. We had adjacent *kuṭīs* in a far corner of the monastery and had become friends, offering each other companionship and support in this way, basically relaxing and goofing off. So you can imagine how surprised and guilty we felt when Ajahn Chah himself suddenly appeared on the path to the *kuṭī*, calling out and beckoning with his hand! We thought we were in for a scolding for not meditating diligently, but Ajahn Chah didn't seem bothered at all, he wasn't telling us to stop talking, but calling to us, 'Come here, come here!'

It transpired that Ajahn Chah was taking time off from being the resident sage of Wat Pah Pong, receiving a constant stream of visitors at his *kuṭī*, and had decided to go hunting for monitor lizards instead! Having just spotted one in the vicinity, he had come to enlist our help, patiently miming an explanation of how to fix a string snare to the end of a bamboo pole. Ajahn Chah was very fond of the forest chickens, which he would feed with rice in the area around his own *kuṭī*. He wanted to protect them from their natural enemy, the large monitor lizards which liked to eat their eggs.

So there followed what turned out to be a hilarious scene of two rather clumsy, inexperienced Westerners, goaded on by an enthusiastic Ajahn Chah, their adopted spiritual guide, thrashing around in the forest trying to catch a big lizard – hardly the sort of thing that I had imagined writing home about! We were quite hopeless, of course, and eventually gave up without catching anything, but not before having a good laugh at ourselves.

What struck me most about this little episode was the contrast between Ajahn Chah the lizard hunter, displaying a very natural spontaneity and down-to-earth, almost childlike simplicity and humour, and the awe-inspiring formality of his role as head of a large important monastery, which up to that point was all I had ever seen of him. This had the effect of undermining many of my own pre-conceptions regarding what a great enlightened teacher was supposed to be like, and helped me to see that Ajahn Chah was actually very natural and quite funny. So I was able to feel less intimidated and more relaxed in being around him.

I spent the *Vassa* of that year as a *pa-khao* with Ajahn Chah, when he unexpectedly decided to leave Wat Pah Pong for the monastery in his home village, Wat Gor Nork, three kilometres away. I was the most junior of the four foreign disciples who accompanied Ajahn Chah at that time for what turned out to be a unique Rains Retreat. He gave some very profound Dhamma talks during this *Vassa*, in response to specific questions by more senior Western monks who took advantage of his increased accessibility in such a small place. Most of this was over my head at the time as my Thai was still pretty minimal, and I was for the most part preoccupied with various chores: cleaning spittoons, etc., such was my lowly position.

Ajahn Chah had come to this little monastery specifically to renovate it, and soon set about building a new *sāla*. He was often to be seen supervising the work in progress, strutting around with his big walking-stick, barking out comments and commands in a most imperious manner, displaying what appeared to be dissatisfaction, irritation or even anger. It was really quite intimidating to watch and I was starting to get a bit put off by it all, when Ajahn Chah seemed to notice that I was having a few doubts about this performance. He looked across at me and by way of reassurance pointed to the centre of his chest and said, 'Nothing here; nothing here!' I realized then that he was actually a consummate actor and could display behaviour without being at all affected by it. He was simply doing what was necessary to get the right response from the village workers, who are culturally conditioned to respond to that kind of expression of authority. Another time I witnessed him metamorphose into a really friendly, jovial old uncle or grandfather in response to a visiting family group – a most saccharine performance that at the time struck me as transparently artificial. But on reflection I could see that it was in fact just right for those people in that situation, and they departed happy and uplifted.

Through experiences like these I learned to let go of fixed views about how supposedly enlightened people should or should not act. Ajahn Chah was very skilful in adapting to circumstances for the sake of inspiring or teaching others, and this indicated a highly developed mind. But an unen-lightened observer of such outward behaviour cannot see the true quality of a mind like that. The purity or lack of defilement cannot be seen directly; all that can be seen is an apparently normal person displaying normal character-istics and reactions. So we should be very cautious about jumping to conclusions or passing judgements based on such superficial observations. As the Buddha pointed out, it is very difficult for an unenlightened person to know the quality of a wise person. It needs keen observation over a long period of time – a very important point.

Visiting Ajahn Chah back at Wat Pah Pong after that *Vassa*, I found him directing a contingent of young conscript soldiers who had come to help clean up the monastery, sweeping, picking up leaves, etc. There he was, sitting in his wicker chair, waving his stick and bellowing orders left, right and centre. Seeing it was me who had come to sit beside him under his *kuṭī*, he made an oblique reference to the previous encounter at Wat Gor Nork by leaning over and saying with a little grin, 'You can't talk to Westerners like that, can you?'

I was impressed by how much he seemed to understand the character of Westerners and the problems they had in undertaking the monastic training. Although he spoke most of the time in the appropriate way for Thais – who are conditioned to respond to authority like that – yet he was adaptable and quick enough to pick up the ways of dealing with Westerners, even those who couldn't understand his language. The villagers were always amazed by how Ajahn

Chah, who had very little in the way of formal education or worldly sophistication, could actually teach so many Western disciples without even speaking English. Ajahn Chah would simply point out that they themselves were raising chickens and buffalo all the time without knowing their language, and were managing all right!

He was very observant and could quite accurately assess the personality of approaching newcomers by watching their faces, their postures, the way they walked, etc. Before they had even sat down or said anything, Ajahn Chah would make a remark to those present, such as, 'This one's full of doubt!' which subsequent conversation would reveal to be true.

More than anything else, I think it was probably his humour that made him attractive to Westerners, for whom conceit, views and attachment to all sorts of worldly knowledge and sophistication could be serious obstructions. But Ajahn Chah would have means of deflating all that in a humorous way. It's very difficult to point out somebody's defilements in an acceptable way that doesn't cause offence or inspire resistance or rejection. But Westerners generally have a rather sarcastic sense of humour, and Ajahn Chah would play on that with his own wit and make people aware of their own faults in a very funny way, which would in turn endear him to them even more.

Most of the time I was actually with Ajahn Chah, I didn't understand Thai very well at all, and just as I was getting competent in the language, he got sick and was incapacitated to the point of being unable to speak. But although the tapes and books produced in later times made me aware of what I had missed experiencing personally, I feel no regret about it, because after being a monk for so many years now, I really believe that the initiation into spiritual life of those early years gave me something that has sustained me right up to the present. Basically, the simple conviction that this is right; it works, it is all you need. This conviction sprang directly from my own experience of Ajahn Chah's example; this person who seemed to have such cast-iron integrity, who conveyed complete certainty and a kind of natural authority that commanded respect. Confronted almost daily by all kinds of people, problems and questions, he was quite unshaken from this position of inner certainty and calm. No one could upset him or make him change his position, and this was most impressive. I had never seen anyone so constant, and it seemed to be proof that he was operating on quite a different level from the average person.

So although I can't really claim to have had profound discussions or a deep, personal connection with Ajahn Chah, just the constancy of his presence was enough to anchor me to the principles of the training he taught. And it inspired great confidence to have an example of someone who had achieved such results from the practice, who embodied the Dhamma and lived it all the time. Consequently, I never really had doubts about it or any problems in surrendering myself to it. I had never had a teacher before or much understanding of what that might imply, and was also a fairly critical person with a rather cynical bent. But the example of Ajahn Chah himself made the surrender of opinions and preferences, the endurance of simplicity and austerity, the tribulations of diet and climate, etc. a joy to undertake.

Without such an example as a constant reminder, it's very easy to remain stuck in one's own views and opinions, which is a major obstacle to success in training. Westerners especially have problems because they know so much. They know that there are other teachers, other traditions and books all over the place, and they can just get lost, never really grasping the point of it all. Ajahn Chah would say, 'Don't read books. Don't write home more than twice a year. You've come here to die!' The idea of living in the forest and being simple really appealed to me, as my character naturally disposes me to be that way. It was no great wrench to take up the forest life.

It's often assumed that living with a teacher means having an in-depth personal rapport, characterized by weighty discussions of profound topics pertaining to spiritual life and the highest goals thereof. But that's not necessarily the case. You never really enter spiritual life whole-heartedly until you surrender yourself, surrender views and opinions. Ajahn Chah's genius was in his ability to point this out, orchestrating an environment or training situation in which people could become aware of their own defilements and learn not to believe their own thinking. This is incredibly important. Without the example of someone who has done it; who lives it, it's really difficult to give up self-concern. I never had any problems wondering whether I should be doing this or whether I should go somewhere else. Inspired by Ajahn

Chah's example, I just got on with it. I didn't see any point in going anywhere else.

Eventually you verify the teaching through your own practice, and you realize how things change. Your habits change; your character changes. Your defilements get less. Life gets easier and your mind is more peaceful. Everything Ajahn Chah has been saying is true!

Ajahn Chandapālo

My experience with Ajahn Chah is very limited because I only saw him one time before he got really sick, when he could still walk and talk and function normally. While I was studying in Scotland he was invited to visit Edinburgh, and he was with Ajahn Sumedho and Ajahn Pabhākaro. He had just arrived that evening, and he stayed overnight and left the following day. There was a meeting with a few people. He didn't give a talk, just questions and answers, and I can't remember what he said, but it did leave an impression. I remember him as someone totally at ease and just completely normal. There was nothing really outstanding, he was just someone who was 'right there'. There was no kind of pretence or play-acting; he was just who he was.

It was just a short meeting, a short meditation. Afterwards he answered questions and I saw him for an hour or so. I was still quite new to practice and Buddhism. The only monk I'd met before was Ajahn Sumedho, so it felt like a very important and fortunate thing to be able to meet his teacher as well. I felt very much in awe, you know – Ajahn Chah!

We were waiting for them to arrive and I happened to be just outside in the corridor when he came. I remember feeling quite shy and embarrassed, not knowing how to behave. So I just raised my hands in *añjalī* (a gesture of respect) as he walked past – he was really short and walking with a stick. And he stopped and looked up at me, and then carried on.

Q: Do you remember what year this was in?

A: It must have been 1979. I remember him sitting in a chair and just looking around, tapping things with his stick. I felt there was kindness, a good feeling from just being in his presence. It was a long time ago and very brief, but what stands out is that feeling of the goodness of his presence, and that he was someone who was very much at ease.

I've always enjoyed his teachings that have been published in books, like '*Bodhinyana*' and 'A Taste of Freedom', very inspiring. There's an apparent simplicity in them, but also the depth and profundity of his wisdom comes across. And even though you can read them many times, there's still something that reaches and touches you – something inspiring.

Ajahn Karuṇiko

I met Luang Por Chah in England. He came to the Hampstead Vihāra in 1979, when I was still a layman. One of the things I noticed was just the sense of happiness of Luang Por Chah, his joy and happiness and the effect that had on my mind. It made me feel very happy to be around him. One of the most interesting things about that time was that I had been meditating for maybe 18 months and it was very difficult, there was pain, restlessness. But then Luang Por Chah arrived at the Vihāra, and my mind was very calm and peaceful. So I'd go every night because my meditation was very good when he was there. That was very interesting – just the power of his presence and my mind went calm. Usually it wasn't calm, because in my early days of meditation, sitting wasn't easy. But it was easy to sit when he was there.

Then I think just the power of his *mettā* affected me – this nice feeling in the heart. So I really enjoyed just being around him. It was a very special time, that week he was there; I'd go every night. It was interesting too that even if he was downstairs in the Vihāra, still my meditation was good, even when he was not in the room – incredible. I noticed that when he left to go back to Thailand.

He used to tease people; ask people questions and tease them a little bit. So when I sat there and I was at his feet, just in awe of this wonderful man, he looked down at me and said, 'What do you think it would be like to sit there for one whole hour without one thought coming into your mind?', I thought, 'Oh, very enlightened!' But he said, 'Like a stone!' and I couldn't answer that! Being around him when he came to the Hampstead Vihāra when I was a layman was a very wonderful experience. And that's more or less the only time I really was near to Luang Por Chah when he was well.

Part II

FOREST SANGHA NEWSLETTER ARTICLES

2

GRATITUDE
TO AJAHN CHAH

Issue 9, published in July 1989.

June 17th was the 71st birthday of, Venerable Ajahn Chah, spiritual teacher of over 80 forest monasteries in Thailand, Britain and around the world. As is customary in the monasteries in England, the day's practice was offered in gratitude to him and for his well-being. In this Newsletter we present, through some reflections, an occasion for readers to recollect what he has made possible for all of us.

Venerable Jayasāro was formally abbot at Wat Pah Nanachat. In 1988 he visited the UK as a translator for Venerable Chao Khun Paññananda. The following reflections on Ajahn Chah's life are taken from a talk given at Amaravati Buddhist Centre in June of that year.

My own first meeting with Ajahn Chah was on the full moon of December 1978. I had spent the Rains Retreat of that year as an eight-precept lay person with Ajahn Sumedho at

Oakenholt in England. After the retreat I went out to Thailand. When I arrived at Wat Pah Pong, Venerable Pamutto, an Australian monk resident there at the time, took me to see Ajahn Chah. He was sitting under his *kuṭī* having a drink. He looked at me and smiled very warmly. He held out the drink he had in his hand, so I crawled over and took it. As I returned to my place I found there were tears welling up in my eyes. I was emotionally overcome for quite a while. Since that day I don't think I have ever wanted to leave the monastery or do anything except be a disciple of Ajahn Chah.

People often presumed there would be a problem with language for Westerners who wanted to stay at the monastery, but this was not the case. Someone once asked Ajahn Chah: 'Luang Por, how do you teach all your Western disciples? Do you speak English or French? Do you speak Japanese or German?' 'No,' replied Ajahn Chah. 'Then how do they all manage?' he asked. 'Householder', Ajahn Chah enquired, 'at your home do you have water buffaloes?' 'Yes, Luang Por' was the reply. 'Do you have any cows, or dogs, or chickens?' 'Yes, Luang Por.' 'Tell me', Luang Por asked, 'do you speak waterbuffalo: do you speak cow?' 'No,' the householder replied. 'Well, how do they all manage?'

Language was not so important to Luang Por. He knew how to see through the exterior trappings of language and culture. He could see how all minds basically revolve around the same old centres of greed, hatred and delusion. His method of training was one of pointing directly at the way our minds work. He was always showing us how craving gives rise to suffering – actually allowing us to see the Four Noble Truths directly. And for him, the way of exposing desires was to frustrate them. In his vocabulary, the words 'to teach' and 'to torment' were more or less interchangeable.

Such training as this can only take place if everyone in the monastery has great confidence in the teacher. If there is the slightest suspicion that he might be doing it out of aversion or desire for power, there wouldn't be any benefit. In Ajahn Chah's case everyone could see that he had the greatest courage and fortitude, and so could trust that he was doing it out of compassion.

Primarily he would teach about letting go. But he also taught a lot about what to do when we can't let go. 'We endure', he would say. Usually people could appreciate intellectually about letting go, but when faced with obstacles they couldn't do it. The teaching of patient endurance was a central aspect of the way that he taught. He continually changed routines around in the monastery so you wouldn't become stuck in ruts. As a result you kept finding yourself not quite knowing where you stood. And he would always be there watching, so you couldn't be too heedless. This is one of the great values of living with a teacher; one feels the need to be mindful.

In looking into Ajahn Chah's early life, it was inspiring for me to find just how many problems he had. Biographies of some great masters leave you with the impression that they were perfectly pure from the age of eight or nine – that they didn't have to work at their practice. But for Ajahn

Chah practice was very difficult. For one thing, he had a lot of sensual desire. He also had a great deal of desire for beautiful requisites, such as his bowl and robes, etc. He made a resolution in working with these tendencies that he would never ask for anything, even if it was permitted to do so by the Discipline. He related once how his robes had been falling to bits; his under-robe was worn paper-thin, so he had to walk very carefully lest it split. Then one day he heedlessly squatted down and it tore completely. He didn't have any cloth to patch it, but remembered the foot-wiping cloths in the Meeting Hall. So he took them away, washed them and patched his robe with them.

In later times when he had disciples, he excelled in skilful means for helping them; he had had so many problems himself. In another story, he related how he made a resolution to really work with sensual desire. He resolved that for the three-month Rains Retreat he would not look at a woman. Being very strong-willed, he was able to keep to this. On the last day of the retreat many people came to the monastery to make offerings. He thought, 'I've done it now for three months, let's see what happens.' He looked up, and at that moment there was a young woman right in front of him. He said the impact was like being hit by lightning. It was then that he realized mere sense restraint, although essential, was not enough. No matter how restrained one might be regarding the eyes, ears, nose, tongue, body, and mind, if there wasn't wisdom to understand the actual nature of desire, then freedom from it was impossible.

He was always stressing the importance of wisdom, not just restraint, but mindfulness and contemplation. Throwing oneself into practice with great gusto and little reflective ability may result in a strong concentration practice, but one eventually ends up in despair. Monks practising like this usually come to a point where they decide that they don't have what it takes to 'break through' in this lifetime, and disrobe. He emphasized that continuous effort was much more important than making a great effort for a short while, only to let it all slide. Day in, day out; month in, month out; year, in year out: that is the real skill of the practice.

What is needed in mindfulness practice, he taught, is a constant awareness of what one is thinking, doing or saying. It is not a matter of being on retreat or off retreat, or of being in a monastery or out wandering on *tudong*; it's a matter of constancy: 'What am I doing now; why am I doing it?' Constantly looking to see what is happening in the present moment. Is this mind state coarse or refined?' At the beginning of practice, he said, our mindfulness is intermittent, like water dripping from a tap. But as we continue, the intervals between the drips lessen and eventually they become a stream. This stream of mindfulness is what we are aiming for.

It was noticeable that he did not talk a lot about levels of enlightenment or the various states of concentration absorption (*jhāna*). He was aware of how people tend to attach to these terms and conceive of practice as going from this stage to that. Once someone asked him if such and such a person was an *arahant* – was enlightened. He answered, 'If they are then they are, if they're not, then they're not; you are what you are, and you're not like them. So just do your own practice.' He was very short with such questions.

When people asked him about his own attainments, he never spoke praising himself or making any claim whatsoever. When talking about the foolishness of people, he wouldn't say, 'You think like this and you think like that', or 'You do this and you do that.' Rather, he would always say, 'We do this and we do that.' The skill of speaking in such a personal manner meant that those listening regularly came away feeling he was talking directly to them. Also, it often happened that people would come with personal problems they wanted to discuss with him, and that very same evening he would give a talk covering exactly that subject.

In setting up his monasteries, he took a lot of his ideas from the great meditation teacher Venerable Ajahn Mun, but also from other places he encountered during his years of wandering. Always he laid great emphasis on a sense of community. In one section of the *Mahāparinibbāna Sutta*[1] the Buddha speaks about the welfare of the Sangha being dependent on meeting frequently in large numbers, in harmony, and on discussing things together. Ajahn Chah stressed this a lot.

The *Bhikkhu* Discipline (the *Vinaya*) was to Ajahn Chah a very important tool for training. He had found it so in his own practice. Often he would give talks on it until one or two o'clock in the morning; the bell would then ring at three for

---

[1] Dīgha Nikāya 16.

morning chanting. Monks were sometimes afraid to go back to their *kuṭīs* lest they couldn't wake up, so they would just lean against a tree.

Especially in the early days of his teaching things were very difficult. Even basic requisites like lanterns and torches were rare. In those days the forest was dark and thick with many wild and dangerous animals. Late at night you could hear the monks going back to their huts making a loud noise, stomping and chanting at the same time, On one occasion twenty torches were given to the monastery, but as soon as the batteries ran out they all came back into the stores, as there were no new batteries to replace them.

Sometimes Ajahn Chah was very harsh on those who lived with him. He admitted himself that he had an advantage over his disciples. He said that when his mind entered *samādhi* concentration for only 30 minutes, it could be the same as having slept all night. Sometimes he talked for literally hours, going over and over the same things again and again, telling the same story hundreds of times. For him, each time was as if it was the first. He would be sitting there giggling and chuckling away, and everybody else would be looking at the clock and wondering when he would let them go.

It seemed that he had a special soft spot for those who suffered a lot; this often meant the Western monks. There was one English monk, Venerable Ṭhitabho, to whom he gave a lot of attention; that means he tormented him terribly. One day there was a large gathering of visitors to the monastery, and as often happened, Ajahn Chah was praising the Western monks to the Thais as a way of teaching them. He was saying how clever the Westerners were, all the things they could do and what good disciples they were. 'All', he said, 'except this one', pointing to Venerable Ṭhitabho. 'He's really stupid.' Another day he asked Venerable Ṭhitabho, 'Do you get angry when I treat you like this?' Venerable Ṭhitabho replied, 'What use would it be? It would be like getting angry at a mountain.'

Several times people suggested to Ajahn Chah that he was like a Zen master. 'No I'm not', he would say, 'I'm like Ajahn Chah.' There was a Korean monk visiting once who liked to ask him *koans*. Ajahn Chah was completely baffled; he thought they were jokes. You could see how it was necessary to know the rules of the game before you could give the right answers. One day this monk told Ajahn Chah the Zen story about the flag and the wind, and asked, 'Is it the flag that blows or is it the wind?' Ajahn Chah answered, 'It's neither; it's the mind.' The Korean monk thought that was wonderful and immediately bowed to Ajahn Chah. But then Ajahn Chah said he'd just read the story in the Thai translation of Hui Neng.

Many of us tend to confuse complexity with profundity, so Ajahn Chah liked to show how profundity was in fact simplicity. The truth of impermanence is the most simple thing in the world, and yet it is the most profound. He really emphasized that. He said the key to living in the world with wisdom is a regular recollection of the changing nature of things. 'Nothing is sure,' he would constantly remind us. He was always using this expression in Thai – '*Mai nair!*' –

meaning 'uncertain'. He said this teaching, 'It's not certain', sums up all the wisdom of Buddhism. He emphasized that in meditation, 'We can't go beyond the hindrances unless we really understand them.' This means knowing their impermanence.

Often he talked about 'killing the defilements', and this also meant 'seeing their impermanence'. 'Killing defilements' is an idiomatic expression in the meditative Forest Tradition of north-east Thailand. It means that by seeing with penetrative clarity the actual nature of defilements, you go beyond them.

While it was considered the 'job' of a *bhikkhu* in this tradition to be dedicated to formal practice, that didn't mean there wasn't work to do. When work needed doing you did it. And you didn't make a fuss. Work is not any different from formal practice if one knows the principles properly. The same principles apply in both cases, as the same body and mind are active. And in Ajahn Chah's monasteries, when the monks worked, they really worked. One time he wanted a road built up to Wat Tum Saeng Pet mountain monastery, and the Highways Department offered to help. But before long they pulled out, so Ajahn Chah took the monks up there to do it. Everybody worked from three o'clock in the afternoon until three o'clock the next morning. A rest was allowed until just after five, when they would head off down the hill to the village on alms-round. After the meal they could rest again until three, before starting work once more. But nobody saw Ajahn Chah take a rest; he was busy receiving people who came to visit. And when it was time for work he didn't just direct it. He joined in the heavy lifting, carrying rocks alongside everyone else. That was always very inspiring for the monks to see: hauling water from the well, sweeping and so on, he was always there, right up until the time when his health began to fail.

Ajahn Chah wasn't always popular in his province in north-east Thailand, even though he did bring about many major changes in the lives of the people. There was a great deal of animism and superstition in their belief systems. Very few people practised meditation, out of fear that it would drive them crazy. There was more interest in magical powers and psychic phenomena than in Buddhism. A lot of killing of animals was done in the pursuit of merit. Ajahn Chah was often very outspoken on such issues, so he had many enemies.

Nevertheless, there were always many who loved him, and it was clear that he never played on that. In fact, if any of his disciples were getting too close, he would send them away. Sometimes monks became attached to him, and he promptly sent them off to some other monastery. Charismatic as he was, he always stressed the importance of the Sangha – of community spirit.

I think it was because Ajahn Chah was 'nobody in particular' that he could be anybody he chose. If he felt it was necessary to be fierce, he could be that. If he felt that somebody would benefit from warmth and kindness, then he would give them. You had the feeling he would be whatever was helpful for the person he was with. And he was very clear about the proper understanding of conventions. Someone once asked about the relative merits of *arahants* and *bodhisattvas*. He answered, 'Don't be an *arahant*, don't be a *bodhisattva*, don't be anything at all. If you are an *arahant* you will suffer, if you are a *bodhisattva* you will suffer, if you are anything at you will suffer.' I had the feeling that Ajahn Chah wasn't anything at all. The quality in him which inspired awe was the light of Dhamma he reflected; it wasn't exactly him as a person.

So since first meeting Ajahn Chah, I have had an unshakeable conviction that this way is truly possible – it works – it is good enough. And I've found a willingness to acknowledge that if there are any problems, it's me who is creating them. It's not the form and it's not the teachings. This appreciation made things a lot easier. It's important that we are able to learn from all the ups and downs we have in practice. It's important that we come to know how to be 'a refuge unto ourselves'– to see clearly for ourselves. When I consider the morass of selfishness and foolishness my life could have been, and then reflect on the teachings and benefits I've received, I find I really want to dedicate my life to being a credit to my teacher. This reflection has been a great source of strength. This is one form of *Sanghānussati*, 'recollection of the Sangha' – recollection of the great debt we owe our teachers.

So I trust that you may find this is of some help in your practice.

3

LIVING WITH LUANG POR

Issue 13, published in July 1990. Further recollections by those who knew him.

Paul Breiter

Formerly Ven. Varapañño, writes of his early contact with Ajahn Chah (c. 1970):

One cold afternoon as we swept the monastery grounds with long-handled brooms, I thought how nice it would be, what a simple thing it really was, if we could have a sweet drink of sugary coffee or tea after working like that, to warm the bones and give us a little energy for meditation at night.

I had heard that Western monks in the forest tend to get infatuated with sweets, and finally the dam burst for me. One morning on *piṇḍapat*, from the moment I walked out of the gate of the Wat to the moment I came back about one and a half hours later, I thought continually about sugar, candy, sweets, chocolate. Finally I sent a letter asking a lay supporter in Bangkok to send me some palm-sugar cakes. And I waited. The weeks went by. One day I went to town with a layman to get medicine. We stopped by the Post Office and my long-awaited package was there. It was huge, and ants were already at it.

When I got back to the Wat, I took the box to my *kuṭī* and opened it. There were 20-25 pounds of palm and sugarcane cakes. I went wild, stuffing them down until my stomach ached. Then I thought I should share them (otherwise I might get very sick!), so I put some aside and took the rest to Ajahn Chah's *kuṭī*. He had the bell rung, all the monks and novices came, and everyone enjoyed a rare treat.

That night I ate more; and the next morning I couldn't control myself. The sugar cakes were devouring me; my blessing started to seem like a curse. So I took the cakes in a plastic bag and decided to go round the monks' *kuṭīs* and gave them away.

For a start I fell down my stairs and bruised myself nicely. The wooden stairs can get slippery in cold weather, and I wasn't being very mindful in my guilty, distressed state of mind.

The first *kuṭī* I went to had a light on inside, but I called and there was no answer. Finally, after I'd called several times and waited, the monk timidly asked who it was (I didn't yet understand how strong fear of ghosts is among those people). I offered him some sugar, and he asked me why I didn't want to keep it for myself. I tried to explain about my defiled state of mind. He took one (it was hard to get them to take much, as it is considered to be in very bad taste to display one's desire or anger).

I repeated this with a few others, having little chats along the way. It was getting late, and although I hadn't unloaded all the sugar cakes, I headed back to my *kuṭī*. My flashlight batteries were almost dead, so I lit matches to try to have a view of the path – there were lots of poisonous things creeping and crawling around in the forest. I ran into some army ants and experienced my first fiery sting. I got back to my *kuṭī* feeling very foolish. In the morning I took the rest of the cakes and gave them to one of the senior monks, who I felt would have the wisdom and self-discipline to be able to handle them.

But my heart grew heavy. I went to see Ajahn Chah in the afternoon to confess my sins. I felt like it was all over for me, there was no hope left. He was talking with an old monk. I made the customary three prostrations, sat down and waited. When he acknowledged me, I blurted out, 'I'm impure, my mind is soiled, I'm no good...' He looked very concerned. 'What is it?' he asked. I told him my story. Naturally he was amused, and within a few minutes I realized that he had me laughing. I was very light-hearted; the world was no longer about to end. In fact, I had forgotten about my burden. This was one of his most magical gifts. You could feel so burdened and depressed and hopeless, and after being around him for a few minutes it all vanished, and you found yourself laughing. Sometimes you only needed to go and sit down at his *kuṭī* and be around him as he spoke with others. Even when he was away I would get a 'contact high' of peacefulness as soon I got near his *kuṭī* to clean up or to sweep leaves.

He said, 'In the afternoon, when water-hauling is finished, you come here and clean up.' My first reaction was, 'He's got a lot of nerve, telling me to come and wait on him.' But apart from being one of my duties, it was a foot in the door and a privilege. Through it, I was to start seeing that there was a way of life in the monastery which is rich, structured and harmonious. And at the centre of it all is the teacher, who is someone to be relied on.

Finally, he asked why I was so skinny. Immediately, one of the monks who was there told him that I took a very small ball of rice at meal-time. Did I not like the food? I told him I just couldn't digest much of the sticky rice, so I kept cutting down. I had come to accept it as the way it was, thinking I was so greedy that eating less and less was a virtue. But he was concerned. Did I feel tired? Most of the time I had little strength, I admitted. 'So', he said, 'I'm going to put you on a special diet for a while – just plain rice gruel and fish sauce to start with. You eat a lot of it, and your stomach will stretch out. Then we'll go to boiled rice, and finally to sticky rice. I'm a doctor', he added. (I found out later on that he actually was an accomplished herbalist, as well as having knowledge of all the illnesses to which monks are prone). He told me not to push myself too much. If I didn't have any strength, I didn't have to carry water, etc.

That was when the magic really began. That was when he was no longer just Ajahn Chah to me. He became Luang Por, 'Venerable Father'.

Ajahn Munindo

A visit from Luang Por:

There was a very difficult period in my training in Thailand, after I had already been a monk for about four years. As a result of a motorbike accident I had had before I was ordained, and a number of years of sitting in bad posture, my knees seized up. The doctors in Bangkok said it was severe arthritis, but nothing that a small operation couldn't fix. They said it would take two or three weeks. But after two months and three operations I was still hardly walking. There had been all kinds of complications: scar tissue, three lots of general anaesthetic and the hot season was getting at me; my mind was really in a state. I was thinking, 'My whole life as a monk is ruined. Whoever heard of a Buddhist monk who can't sit cross-legged?' Every time I saw somebody sitting cross-legged I'd feel angry. I was feeling terrible, and my mind was saying, 'It shouldn't be like this; the doctor shouldn't have done it like that; the monks' rules shouldn't be this way ....' It was really painful, physically and mentally. I was in a very unsatisfactory situation.

Then I heard that Ajahn Chah was coming down to Bangkok. I thought if I went to see him he might be able to help in some way. His presence was always very uplifting.

When I visited him I couldn't bow properly; he looked at me and asked, 'What are you up to?' I began to complain. 'Oh, Luang Por', I said, 'It's not supposed to be this way. The doctors said two weeks and it has been two months ...' I was really wallowing. With a surprised expression on his face he said to me, very powerfully, 'What do you mean, it shouldn't be this way? If it shouldn't be this way, it wouldn't be this way!'

That really did something to me. He pointed to exactly what I was doing that was creating the problem. There was no question about the fact of the pain; the problem was my denying that fact, and that was something I was doing. This is not just a theory. When someone offers us the reflection of exactly what we are doing, we are incredibly grateful, even if at that time we feel a bit of a twit.

Ajahn Sumedho

An incident from his early days with Ajahn Chah (c. 1967-69):

In those days I was a very junior monk, and one night Ajahn Chah took us to a village fete – I think Satimanto was there at the time.

Now, we were all very serious practitioners and didn't want any kind of frivolity or foolishness; so of course going to a village fete was the last thing we wanted to do, because in these villages they love loudspeakers.

Anyway, Ajahn Chah took Satimanto and I to this village fete, and we had to sit up all night with all the raucous sounds of the loudspeakers going and monks giving talks all night long. I kept thinking, 'Oh, I want to get back to my cave. Green skin monsters and ghosts are much better than this.' I noticed that Satimanto (who was incredibly serious) was looking angry and critical, and very unhappy. So we sat there looking miserable, and I thought, 'Why does Ajahn Chah bring us to these things?' Then I began to see for myself. I remember sitting there thinking, 'Here I am getting all upset over this. Is it that bad? What's really bad is what I'm making out of it, what's really miserable is my mind. Loudspeakers and noise, distraction and sleepiness – all that, one can really put up with. It's that awful thing in my mind that hates it, resents it and wants to leave.'

That evening I could really see what misery I could create in my mind over things that one can bear. I remember that as a very clear insight of what I thought was miserable and what really is miserable. At first I was blaming the people and the loudspeakers, and the disruption, the noise and the discomfort, I thought that was the problem. Then I realized that it wasn't – it was my mind that was miserable.

Sister Candasiri

Sister Candasiri first met Luang Por Chah while still a laywoman, during his second visit to England in 1979:

For me one of the most striking things about Luang Por Chah was the effect of his presence on those around him. Watching Ajahn Sumedho – who hitherto had been for me a somewhat awe-inspiring teacher – sit at his feet with an attitude of sheer delight, devotion and adoration lingers in the mind as a memory of extraordinary sweetness. Ajahn Chah would tease him, 'Maybe it's time for you to come back to Thailand!' Everyone gasped inwardly: 'Is he serious?'

Later on a visitor, a professional flautist, began to ask about music. 'What about Bach? Surely there's nothing wrong with that – much of his music is very spiritual, not at all worldly.' (It was a question that interested me greatly). Ajahn Chah looked at her, and when she had finished he said quietly, 'Yes, but the music of the peaceful heart is much, much more beautiful.'

Ajahn Santacitto

Recollecting his own first meeting with Ajahn Chah:

From the very first meeting with Ajahn Chah, I couldn't help but be aware of how powerful a force was emanating from this person. I had just arrived at the monastery with a friend, and neither of us spoke much Thai, so the possibility of talking with and hearing Dhamma from Ajahn Chah was very limited. I was considering taking ordination as a monk mainly in order to learn about meditation, rather than from any serious inclination towards religious practice.

It happened that just at that time, a group of local villagers came to ask him to perform a certain traditional ceremony which involved a great deal of ritual. The laymen bowed down before the Master, then they got completely covered over with a white cloth, and then holy water was brought out and candles were dripped into it, while the monks did the chanting. And young lad that I was, very science-minded, rather iconoclastic by nature, I found this all rather startling, and wondered just what I was letting myself in for. Did I really want to become one of these guys and do this kind of thing?

So I just started to look around, watching this scene unfold before me, until my eye caught Ajahn Chah's, and what I saw on his face was very unexpected: there was the smile of a mischievous young man, as if he were saying, 'Good fun, isn't it!' This threw me a bit; I could no longer think of him as being attached to this kind of ritual, and I began to appreciate his wisdom. But a few minutes later, when the ceremony was over and everyone got up and out from under the cloth, all looking very happy and elated, I noticed that the expression on his face had changed; no sign of that mischievous young lad. And although I couldn't understand a word of Thai, I couldn't help but feel very deeply that quality of compassion in the way he took this opportunity of teaching people who otherwise might not have been open and susceptible. It was seeing how, rather than fighting and resisting social customs with their rites and rituals, he knew how to use them skilfully to help people. I think this is what hooked me.

It happened countless times: people would come to the monastery with their problems, looking for an easy answer, but somehow, whatever the circumstances, his approach never varied. He met everybody with a complete openness, with the 'eyes of a babe', as it seemed to me, no matter who they were. One day a very large Chinese businessman came to visit. He did his rather disrespectful form of bowing, and as he did so his sports shirt slipped over his back pocket, and out stuck a pistol. Carrying a pistol is about the grossest thing you can do when coming to see an Ajahn in a Thai monastery! That really took me aback, but what struck me most of all was that when Ajahn Chah looked at him, there was that same openness, no difference, 'eyes like a babe'. There was a complete openness and willingness to go into the other person's world, to be there, to experience it, to share it with them.

Ajahn Sumedho

Recalling an incident during Luang Por's visit to Britain in 1977:

When Ajahn Chah first visited England, he was invited to a certain woman's home for a vegetarian meal. She obviously had put a lot of effort into creating the most delicious kinds of food. She was bustling about offering this food and looking very enthusiastic. Ajahn Chah was sitting there assessing the situation, and then suddenly he said: 'This is the most delicious and wonderful meal I have ever had!'

That comment was really something, because in Thailand, monks are not supposed to comment on the food. And yet Luang Por suddenly manifested this charming character in complimenting a woman who needed to be complimented, and it made her feel so happy. He had a feeling for the time and place, for the person he was with, for what would be kind. He could step out of the designated role and manifest in ways that were appropriate; he was not actually breaking any rules, but it was out of character. Now, that shows wisdom and the ability to respond to a situation – not to be just rigidly bound within a convention that blinds you.

Paul Breiter

On his visit in 1979, he related that once a Westerner (a layman, I think) came to Wat Pah Pong and asked him if he was an *arahant*. Ajahn Chah told him, 'Your question is a question to be answered. I will answer it like this: I am like a tree in the forest. Birds come to the tree, they will sit on its branches and eat its fruit. To the birds, the fruit may be sweet or sour or whatever. But the tree doesn't know anything about it. The birds say 'sweet' or they say 'sour' – from the tree's point of view this is just the chattering of the birds.'

On that same evening we also discussed the relative virtues of the *arahant* and the *bodhisattva*. He ended our discussion by saying, 'Don't be an arahant. Don't be a Buddha. Don't be anything at all. Being something makes problems. So don't be anything. You don't have to be something, he doesn't have to be something, I don't have to be something ...' He paused, and then said, 'Sometimes when I think about it, I don't want to say anything.'

4

AJAHN CHAH PASSES AWAY

Issue 20, published in April 1992. Venerable Ṭhitapañño offers an account of the events at Wat Pah Pong immediately following Luang Por Chah's death.

On the morning of 16th January, the Sangha in Britain received a brief message from Wat Pah Nanachat to inform us of the death of Luang Por Chah. The Venerable Ajahn had been critically ill, paralyzed and rendered completely incapacitated by brain damage and numerous strokes over the past ten years. Our winter retreat offered us an ideal opportunity to pay honour to his example, reflect upon his teachings and further our practice in the way that he made clear.

It was during a retreat at Wat Keuan that Ajahn Sumedho and the Western Sangha who had gathered there heard that Luang Por Chah had been admitted to Ubon Hospital. Malfunctioning kidneys and heart complications had proved to be beyond the medical skills of the monks nursing him. During the ten years of his illness Luang Por had entered hospital many times, yet on each occasion he had miraculously recovered. However, reports soon began to reach us that his body was refusing to take food and the general state of his health was deteriorating.

Early on the evening of 15th January the doctors at the ICU realized that Luang Por's condition had deteriorated to the extent that he was beyond medical assistance. At 10 p.m. Luang Por was taken by ambulance to his nursing *kuṭī* at Wat Pah Pong, in compliance with his previous request that he might pass away in his own monastery. It was at 5.20 a.m. on 16th January that the body of Luang Par Chah breathed its last, and in an atmosphere of peace the life of a great Buddhist master came to its end.

The attendant monks chanted the reflection that death is the natural consequence of birth and that in the cessation of conditions is peace, then prepared Luang Por's body for the funeral services. As the news of his death spread, people began to arrive to pay their respects. Soon government officials, as representatives of the King, came to perform the initial ceremonies necessary for a royal funeral.

Within hours the corpse was moved to the main *sāla*, where it was laid in an ornately decorated coffin. The coffin was then sealed, and a picture of Luang Por was placed to the left along with different requisites such as his bowl and robes. Wreaths from the King, the Queen and other members of the royal family were placed to the right. In front of the coffin, extensive flower arrangements created the finishing touches.

As the news of Luang Por's death spread, his disciples rushed to the Wat to pay their respects and offer their support with the preparations to receive visitors to the monastery. It was decided that during the 15 days following Luang Por's death a Dhamma practice session would be held, as an offering of remembrance and a focal point around which the many incoming lay and monastic disciples could collect themselves. The Sangha from Wat Pah Nanachat would come over every day at around 5 p.m. and stay until midnight. During this period of 15 days, about 400 monks, 70 nuns and 500 laypeople resided at Wat Pah Pong, practising meditation until midnight, listening to talks on Dhamma themes and participating in various funeral ceremonies. Most of the Sangha were living out under the trees of the forest, using their *glots* (mosquito net umbrellas) as protection from the elements and insects. The monastery became a *glot* village.

Soon a huge open-air restaurant complex sprung up at the entrance to the monastery, serving free food and drink to the enormous numbers of people who began to make their way there from all over Thailand. As the days passed, I began to feel a sense of awe as people streamed into the monastery from early morning to late at night: people of all ages – families, school groups and individuals. In those first few days over 50,000 books were distributed, which gives some indication of the numbers coming. By the fourteenth and fifteenth days, the number of people coming was steadily increasing to over 10,000 per day. As the people entered the monastery, they filed quietly down the road leading to the *sāla*, waiting for an opportunity to enter and bow in respect, and then to sit for a short while before making way for the next group. Meanwhile the monks, nuns and resident laypeople would be sitting in meditation, chanting or listening to a talk. Luang Por Jun led the funeral chanting and various senior monks gave talks. Ajahn Mahā Boowa, the renowned forest meditation master, came over from his own monastery near Udorn to give a Dhamma talk, and commented on the quiet, harmonious atmosphere of the Wat, in contrast to the confusion and noise he had experienced at similar funerals.

A visit from the King's sister at this time seemed to presage the arrival of the King for the fiftieth day ceremonies on 6th March. As always in Buddhism, however, especially in Thailand, nothing is certain. The hundredth day after the death of Luang Por will also be a day of considerable importance.

Because of the arrangements for the hundreds of thousands of people expected to attend the actual burning of Luang Por's body (at similar funerals for famous teachers, up to a million people have attended), and also to find a day suitable for the King, it was decided to hold the funeral early in 1993.

For each of us Luang Por Chah has a personal meaning, depending on our contact with him. I will always wonder and be inspired at the sight of tens of thousands of people coming to Wat Pah Pong, to pay respects to a person who had not spoken for ten years, and with whom most had never had the opportunity to speak. They came to bow before the body of a being whom they recognized as personifying our highest aspiration – a life free from the blindness of self-centred action. Freed of this delusion, the goal of the Buddhist path is fulfilled. For me, the whole occasion demonstrated the breadth and power of the influence of such a being.

5

THE FIFTIETH DAY COMMEMORATION

Issue 20, published in April 1992. Ven. Ñāṇavīro offers a report of the commemorative services at Wat Pah Pong fifty days after the death of Venerable Ajahn Chah.

Wat Pah Nanachat, 6th March

At 1 p.m. 300 laypeople and 200 monks and nuns gathered in the new *sāla*. The floor is polished granite and the walls are partially marbled. Four huge chandeliers hang from the high ceiling. Large garlands of flowers hang from the walls and the shrine is covered in artificial lotuses, which look beautiful. The cry of the wild chickens breaks into the silence – they are all over the Wat!

Ajahn Jun gave a *desanā* at 2 p.m., mentioning the debt of gratitude we all owe to Luang Por Chah. He exhorted us to make an effort to keep up the practices that Luang Por Chah taught. He also talked about the benefits of keeping good standards regarding *sīla* and the monastic conventions, and reminded us that the practice is not in the forest or the Wat, but is the work of the mind in the body. 'So all of Buddhism is right here in this body/mind. Don't let the practice become perfunctory – put life into it. Even though Ajahn Chah is dead, the goodness and virtue that he embodied are still alive.'

At 7 p.m. about 3,000 laypeople and 300 monks and novices gathered in the new *sāla* for the evening chanting. At 9 p.m. Luang Por Paññananda gave a *desanā*. He started by praising Ajahn Chah as one of the great monks of this era, who taught a pure kind of Buddhism, with nothing extraneous. Ajahn Chah had trained a Sangha which could continue, most notably overseas, where monasteries had arisen from his inspiration. They represented a historic occasion in the development of Buddhism.

Luang Por Paññananda commented that Ajahn Chah had taught people to be wise. The way the Pah Pong Sangha was handling the proceedings was a good example: in Thailand some degenerate practices had crept into funeral services, making them an excuse for a party with gambling and alcohol. But the purpose of a funeral is for the study of Dhamma, not for distraction! It's a lesson, a reminder. Even though Ajahn Chah is dead, the goodness and virtue that he embodied are still alive. We must maintain that which he gave to us all: we have to be 'mediums' for Luang Por Chah, channelling his goodness and virtue through our hearts. If we reflect on Luang Por Chah's *mettā*, *sīla* and *paññā* and internalize them, then it's as if he is in our hearts, far better than hanging a medallion with his picture on it around our necks.

Luang Por Paññananda concluded by reflecting that the Buddha left the Dhamma-Vinaya, not an individual, as our teacher, and that his teaching was one of sustaining compassion, wisdom and purity. So our practice is to wish all beings well, refraining from harming others or the environment. Then to have wisdom – whatever we're doing, inquiring as to why are we doing it, what our purpose is and what is the most skilful means. And to dwell in purity – honouring goodness by making body, speech and mind good, associating with good people, and frequenting places of goodness.

Luang Por Paññananda had witnessed a decline in most monasteries after the teacher died, with schisms occurring between the disciples. So we should be careful not to get attached to views, or to wealth and gains, and agree to have regular meetings in order to maintain harmony. Sangha and laity should support all the things that are in line with the way Luang Por Chah taught, and refrain from the things he cautioned us about. We must all help to do this.

The evening continued with different senior monks giving talks. Ajahn Santacitto was next, and his memory of Thai was excellent. They were still talking when we left at 4.45 a.m., but probably finished at dawn with morning *pūjā*.

6

A NOBLE LIFE

Issue 20, published in April 1992.

17th June, 1918 - 16th January 16, 1992

Venerable Ajahn Chah was born on 17th June 1918 in a small village near the town of Ubon Rajathani, north-east Thailand. Between the ages of 9 and 17 he was a *sāmaṇera* (novice monk), during which time he received his basic schooling, before returning to lay life to help his parents on the farm. At the age of 20, however, he decided to resume monastic life, and on 26th April, 1939 he received *upasampadā* (*bhikkhu* ordination).

Ajahn Chah's early monastic life followed a traditional pattern of studying Buddhist teachings and the Pāli scriptural language. In his fifth year as a monk his father fell seriously ill and died, a blunt reminder of the frailty and precariousness of human life. This caused him to think deeply about life's real purpose, for although he had studied extensively and gained some proficiency in Pāli, he seemed no nearer to a personal understanding of the end of suffering. Feelings of disenchantment set in, and finally (in 1946) he abandoned his studies and set off on mendicant pilgrimage.

He walked some 400 km to central Thailand, sleeping in forests and gathering alms-food in the villages on the way. He took up residence in a monastery where the Vinaya was carefully studied and practised. While there he was told about Venerable Ajahn Mun Bhuridatta, a most highly respected meditation master. Keen to meet such an accomplished teacher, Ajahn Chah set off on foot for the north-east in search of him.

At this time Ajahn Chah was wrestling with a crucial problem. He had studied the teachings on morality, meditation and wisdom, which the texts presented in minute and refined detail, but he could not see how they could all actually be put into practice. Ajahn Mun told him that although the teachings are indeed extensive, at their heart they are very simple. With mindfulness established, it is seen that everything arises in the mind; right there is the true path of practice. This succinct and direct teaching was a revelation for Ajahn Chah, and transformed his approach to practice. The way was clear.

For the next seven years Ajahn Chah practised in the style of the austere Forest Tradition, wandering through the countryside in quest of quiet and secluded places for developing meditation. He lived in tiger- and cobra-infested jungles, and even in charnel-grounds, using reflections on death to overcome fear and penetrate to the true meaning of life. In

1954, after years of wandering, he was invited back to his home village. He settled close by, in a fever-ridden haunted forest called 'Pah Pong'. Despite the hardships of malaria, poor shelter and sparse food, disciples gathered around him in increasing numbers. The monastery which is now known as Wat Pah Pong began there, and eventually branch monasteries were also established elsewhere.

The training in Ajahn Chah's monasteries was quite strict and forbidding. Ajahn Chah often pushed his monks to their limits, to test their powers of endurance so that they would develop patience and resolution. He sometimes initiated long and seemingly pointless work projects in order to frustrate their attachment to tranquillity. The emphasis was always on surrender to the way things are, and great stress was placed upon strict observance of the Vinaya.

In 1977 Ajahn Chah was invited to visit Britain by the English Sangha Trust, a charity with the aim of establishing a locally-resident Buddhist Sangha. He took Venerable Sumedho and Venerable Khemadhammo along, and seeing the serious interest there, left them in London at the Hampstead Vihāra. Another two of Ajahn Chah's Western *bhikkhus*, who were then visiting their families in North America, were invited to stay in London to make up a small resident Sangha. He returned to Britain in 1979, at which time the monks were leaving London to begin Chithurst Buddhist Monastery in Sussex. He then went on to America and Canada to visit and teach.

After this trip and again in 1981, Ajahn Chah spent the Rains away from Wat Pah Pong, since his health was failing due to the debilitating effects of diabetes. As his illness worsened, he would use his body as a teaching, a living example of the impermanence of all things. He constantly reminded people to endeavour to find a true refuge within themselves, since he would not be able to teach for very much longer.

Before the end of the 1981 Rains, he was taken to Bangkok for an operation; however, it did little to improve his condition. Within a few months he stopped talking, and gradually he lost control of his limbs until he was completely paralyzed and bedridden. From then on he was diligently nursed and attended by his *bhikkhu* disciples, grateful for the occasion to offer service to the teacher who so patiently and compassionately showed the Way to so many.

7

QUESTIONS & ANSWERS

Issue 22, published in October 1992. Extracts from a conversation between Luang Por Chah and a lay Buddhist.

Q: There are those periods when our hearts happen to be absorbed in things and become blemished or darkened, but we are still aware of ourselves, such as when some form of greed, hatred, or delusion comes up. Although we know that these things are objectionable, we are unable to prevent them from arising. Could it be said that even as we are aware of them, we are providing the basis for increased clinging and attachment, and maybe putting ourselves further back than where we started from?

Luang Por Chah: That's it! You must keep knowing them at that point; that's the method of practice. I mean that simultaneously, we are both aware of them and repelled by them, but lacking the ability to resist them; they just burst forth.

By then it's already beyond your capability to do anything. At that point you have to readjust yourself and then continue contemplation. Don't just give up on them there and then. When you see things arise in that way you tend to get upset or feel regret, but it is possible to say that they are uncertain and subject to change. What happens is that you see these things are wrong, but you are still not ready or able to deal with them. It's as if they are independent entities, the leftover kammic tendencies that are still creating and conditioning the state of the heart. You don't wish to allow the heart to become like that, but it does, and it indicates that your knowledge and awareness are still neither sufficient nor fast enough to keep abreast of things.

You must practise and develop mindfulness as much as you can in order to gain a greater and more penetrating awareness. Whether the heart is soiled or blemished in some way, it doesn't matter; whatever comes up, you should contemplate the impermanence and uncertainty of it. By maintaining this contemplation at each instant that something arises, after some time you will see the impermanence of all sense objects and mental states. Because you see them as such, gradually they will lose their importance, and your clinging and attachment to that which is a blemish on the heart will continue to diminish. Whenever suffering arises, you will be able to work through it and readjust yourself, but you shouldn't give up on this work or set it aside. You must keep up a continuity of effort and try to make your awareness fast enough to keep in touch with the changing mental conditions. It could be said that so far your development of the Path still lacks sufficient energy to overcome the mental defilements; whenever suffering arises, the heart becomes clouded over. But one must keep developing that knowledge and understanding of the clouded heart; this is what you reflect on.

You must really take hold of it and repeatedly contemplate that this suffering and discontentment are just not sure things. They are something that is ultimately impermanent, unsatisfactory, and not-self. Focusing on these three characteristics, whenever these conditions of suffering arise again, you will know them straightaway, having experienced them before.

Gradually, little by little, your practice should gain momentum, and as time passes, whatever sense objects and mental states arise will lose their value in this way. Your heart will know them for what they are and accordingly put them down. When you reach the point where you are able to know things and put them down with ease, they say that the Path has matured internally and you will have the ability to bear down swiftly upon the defilements. From then on there will just be the arising and passing away in this place, the same as waves striking the seashore. When a wave comes in and finally reaches the shoreline, it just disintegrates and vanishes; a new wave comes and it happens again, the wave going no further than the limit of the shoreline. In the same way, nothing will be able to go beyond the limits established by your own awareness.

That's the place where you will meet and come to understand impermanence, unsatisfactoriness and not-self. It is there that things will vanish – the three characteristics of impermanence, unsatisfactoriness and not-self are the same as the seashore, and all sense objects and mental states that are experienced go in the same way as the waves. Happiness is uncertain; it's arisen many times before. Suffering is uncertain; it's arisen many times before. That's the way they are. In your heart you will know that they are like that, they are 'just that much'. The heart will experience these conditions in this way, and they will gradually keep losing their value and importance. This is talking about the characteristics of the heart, the way it is. It is the same for everybody, even the Buddha and all his disciples were like this.

If your practice of the Path matures, it will become automatic and it will no longer be dependent on anything external. When a defilement arises, you will immediately be aware of it and accordingly be able to counteract it. However, that stage when they say that the Path is still neither mature enough nor fast enough to overcome the defilements is something that everybody has to experience – it's unavoidable. But it is at this point that you must use skilful reflection. Don't go investigating elsewhere or trying to solve the problem at some other place. Cure it right there. Apply the cure at that place where things arise and pass away. Happiness arises and then passes away, doesn't it? Suffering arises and then passes away, doesn't it? You will continuously be able to see the process of arising and ceasing, and see that which is good and bad in the heart. These are phenomena that exist and are part of nature. Don't cling tightly to them or create anything out of them at all.

If you have this kind of awareness, then even though you will be coming into contact with things, there will not be any noise. In other words, you will see the arising and passing away of phenomena in a very natural and ordinary way. You will just see things arise and then cease. You will understand the process of arising and ceasing in the light of impermanence, unsatisfactoriness, and not-self.

The nature of the Dhamma is like this. When you can see things as 'just that much', then they will remain as 'just that much.' There will be none of that clinging or holding on – as soon as you become aware of attachment, it will disappear. There will be just the arising and ceasing, and that is peaceful. That it's peaceful is not because you don't hear anything; there is hearing, but you understand the nature of it and don't cling or hold on to anything. This is what is meant by peaceful – the heart is still experiencing sense objects, but it doesn't follow or get caught up in them. A division is made between the heart, sense objects and the defilement; but if you understand the process of arising and ceasing, then there is nothing that can really arise from it – it will end just there.

8

QUESTIONS & ANSWERS II

Issue 23, published in January 1993. The second in a series of extracts from a conversation between Luang Por Chah and a lay Buddhist.

Q: Does one have to practise and gain *samādhi* (concentration) before one can contemplate the Dhamma?

Luang Por Chah: We can say that's correct from one point of view, but from the aspect of practice, *paññā* has to come first. In conventional terms, it's *sīla*, *samādhi* and then *paññā*, but if we are truly practising the Dhamma, then *paññā* comes first. If *paññā* is there from the beginning, it means that we know what is right and what is wrong; and we know the heart that is calm and the heart that is disturbed and agitated.

Talking from the scriptural basis, one has to say that the practice of restraint and composure will give rise to a sense of shame and fear of any form of wrong-doing that potentially may arise. Once one has established the fear of that which is wrong and one is no longer acting or behaving wrongly, then that which is wrong will not be present within one. When there is no longer anything wrong present within, this provides the conditions from which calm will arise in its place. That calm forms a foundation from which *samādhi* will grow and develop over time.

When the heart is calm, that knowledge and understanding which arises from within that calm is called *vipassanā*. This means that from moment to moment there is a knowing in accordance with the truth, and within this are contained different properties. If one was to set them down on paper they would be *sīla*, *samādhi* and *paññā*. Talking about them, one can bring them together and say that these three dhammas form one mass and are inseparable. But if one were to talk about them as different properties, then it would be correct to say *sīla*, *samādhi* and *paññā*.

However, if one was acting in a unwholesome way, it would be impossible for the heart to become calm. So it would be most accurate to see them as developing together, and it would be right to say that this is the way that the heart will become calm. Talking about the practice of *samādhi*: it involves preserving *sīla*, which includes looking after the sphere of one's bodily actions and speech, in order not to do anything which is unwholesome or would lead one to remorse or suffering. This provides the foundation for the practice of calm, and once one has a foundation in calm, this in turn provides a foundation which supports the arising of *paññā*.

In formal teaching they emphasize the importance of *sīla*. *Ādikalyāṇaṃ, majjhekalyāṇaṃ, pariyosānakalyāṇaṃ* – the practice should be beautiful in the beginning, beautiful in the middle and beautiful in the end. This is how it is. Have you ever practised *samādhi*?

I am still learning. The day after I went to see Tan Ajahn at Wat Keu, my aunt brought a book containing some of your teaching for me to read. That morning at work I started to read some passages which contained questions and answers to different problems. In it you said that the most important point was for the heart to watch over and observe the process of cause and effect that takes place within; just to watch and maintain the knowing of the different things that come up.

That afternoon I was practising meditation, and during the sitting the characteristic that appeared was that I felt as though my body had disappeared. I was unable to feel the hands or legs and there were no bodily sensations. I knew that the body was still there, but I couldn't feel it. In the evening I had the opportunity to go and pay respects to Tan Ajahn Tate, and I described to him the details of my experience. He said that these were the characteristics of the heart that appear when it unifies in *samādhi*, and that I should continue practising. I had this experience only once; on subsequent occasions I found that sometimes I was unable to feel only certain areas of the body, such as the hands, whereas in other areas there was still feeling.

Q: Sometimes during my practice I start to wonder whether just sitting and allowing the heart to let go of everything is the correct way to practise; or else should I think over and occupy myself with the different problems or unanswered questions concerning the Dhamma which I still have?

Luang Por Chah: It's not necessary to keep going over or adding anything on at this stage. This is what Tan Ajahn Tate was referring to; one must not repeat or add onto that which is there already. When that particular kind of knowing is present, it means that the heart is calm and it is that state of calm which one must observe. Whatever one feels, whether it feels like there is a body or a self or not, this is not the important point. It should all come within the field of one's awareness. These conditions indicate that the heart is calm and has unified in *samādhi*.

When the heart has unified for a long period a few times, then there will be a change in the conditions and they say that one 'withdraws'. That state is called *appanā samādhi* (absorption), and having entered it, the heart will subsequently withdraw. In fact, although it would not be incorrect to say that the heart withdraws, it doesn't actually withdraw. Another way is to say that it flips back, or that it changes, but the style used by most teachers is to say that once the heart has reached the state of calm, then it will withdraw. However, people get caught up in disagreements over the use of language. It can cause difficulties and one might start to wonder,

'How on earth can it withdraw? This business of withdrawing is just confusing!' It can lead to much foolishness and misunderstanding just because of the language.

What one must understand is that the way to practise is to observe these conditions with *sati-sampajañña* (mindfulness and clear comprehension). In accordance with the characteristic of impermanence, the heart will turn about and withdraw to the level of *upacāra samādhi* (access concentration). If it withdraws to this level, one can gain understanding through awareness of sense impressions and mental states, because at the deeper level (where the mind is fixed with just one object) there is no understanding. If there is awareness at this point, that which appears will be *saṅkhāra* (mental formations). It will be similar to two people having a conversation and discussing the Dhamma together.

One who misunderstands this might feel disappointed that his heart is not really calm, but in fact this dialogue takes place within the confines of the calm and restraint which have developed. These are the characteristics of the heart once it has withdrawn to the level of *upacāra* – there will be the ability to know about and understand different things.

The heart will stay in this state for a period and then it will turn inwards again. In other words, it will turn and go back into the deeper state of calm where it was before; or it is even possible that it might obtain purer and calmer levels of concentrated energy than were experienced before. If it does not reach such a level of concentration, one should merely note the fact and keep observing until the time when the heart withdraws again. Once it has withdrawn, different problems will arise within the heart.

This is the point where one can have awareness and understanding of different things. Here is where one should investigate and examine the different preoccupations and issues which affect the heart, in order to understand and penetrate them. Once these problems are finished with, the heart will gradually move inwards towards the deeper level of concentration again. The heart will stay there and mature, freed from any other work or external impingement. There will just be the one-pointed knowing, and this will prepare and strengthen one's mindfulness until the time to re-emerge is reached.

These conditions of entering and leaving will appear in one's heart during the practice, but this is something that is difficult to talk about. It is not harmful or damaging to one's practice. After a period the heart will withdraw and the inner dialogue will start in that place, taking the form of *saṅkhāra* (mental formations) conditioning the heart. If one doesn't know that this activity is *saṅkhāra*, one might think that it is *paññā*, or that *paññā* is arising. One must see that this activity is fashioning and conditioning the heart, and the most important thing about it is that it is impermanent. One must continually keep control and not allow the heart to start following and believing in all the different creations and stories that it cooks up. All that is just *saṅkhāra*, it doesn't become *paññā*.

The way *paññā* develops is when one listens and knows the heart as the process of creating and conditioning takes it in different directions, and one reflects on the instability and uncertainty of this. The realization of its impermanence will provide the cause by which one can let go of things at that point. Once the heart has let go of things and put them down at that point, it will gradually become more and more calm and steady. One must keep entering and leaving *samādhi* like this, and *paññā* will arise at that point. There one will gain knowledge and understanding.

As one continues to practise, many different kinds of problems and difficulties will tend to arise in the heart; but whatever problems the world or even the universe might bring up, one will be able to deal with them all. One's wisdom will follow them up and find answers for every question and doubt. Wherever one meditates, whatever thoughts come up, whatever happens, everything will be providing the cause for *paññā* to arise. This is a process that will take place by itself, free from external influence.

Paññā will arise like this, but when it does, one should be careful not to become deluded and see it as *saṅkhāra*. Whenever one reflects on things and sees them as impermanent and uncertain, one shouldn't cling or attach to them in any way. If one keeps developing this state, when *paññā* is present in the heart, it will take the place of one's normal way of thinking and reacting, and the heart will become fuller and brighter in the centre of everything. As this happens one knows and understands all things as they really are – one's heart will be able to progress with meditation in the correct way and without being deluded. That is how it should be.

9

RECOLLECTIONS BY JACK KORNFIELD

Issue 27, published in January 1994.

'I was enormously blessed to meet Ajahn Sumedho in 1967 at an old ruined Cambodian temple on a mountain-top in Sakolnakorn, Thailand. With his inspiration I went to see Ajahn Chah at Wat Pah Pong, and eventually entered as a monk in 1969. I left to come back to the USA in 1972, and was re-ordained to live as a monk with Ajahn Chah for a time in 1982. Like all of us who were with him, I could tell many more wonderful stories. Most simply, Ajahn Chah was the wisest man I have ever known, and one of the most delightful, and it has completely changed my life to have him for a teacher.'

Ajahn Chah had four basic levels of teaching, and each one, although at times very difficult for the students, was taught with a lot of humour and a lot of love. Ajahn Chah taught that until we can begin to respect ourselves and our environment, practice doesn't really develop. And that dignity, the ground of practice, comes through surrender, through impeccable discipline. A lot of us in the West understand freedom to mean freedom to do what we want, but I think you can see that to follow the wants of the mind isn't terribly free. It's actually rather troublesome.

A deeper freedom, taught through Dhamma, is the freedom within form: the freedom we can find while relating to another human being, the freedom of being born in a body with its limitations, and the freedom of a tight monastic form. What Ajahn Chah did was create a situation of dignity and demand. He really asked a lot from people, probably more than they'd ever been asked in their whole life – to give, to pay attention, to be wholehearted. Sometimes practice is wonderful: the mind gets so clear that you smell and taste the air in ways that you haven't since you were a child. But sometimes it's difficult. He said, 'That's not the point; the point is somehow to come to inner freedom.'

We used to sit for long hours at times, and the meditation hall for the monks was a stone platform – they don't use cushions in Asia. You have a square cloth like a handkerchief that you put down on the stone to sit on. I remember that when I started, because sitting on the floor was so painful, I would arrive early at the hall and get a place where I could sit next to one of the pillars and lean against it. After about a week of being with Ajahn Chah, he gathered the monks together for an evening talk after the sitting, and he began to talk about how the true practice of Dhamma was to become independent in any circumstance; not to need to lean on things. And then he looked at me.

Sometimes you would sit while he'd talk to someone or receive visitors, and you couldn't leave until you were dismissed. And you'd sit and sit, and you'd look at your mind, and it would go, 'Doesn't he know that we are sitting here? Doesn't he know I'm thirsty or I want to get up?' And he'd be talking away – he knew very well. And you'd sit and sit and just see all the movement of the mind. We would sit for hours. The quality of endurance in the monks' life in the forest, where you just sit and sit and sit, is a very important one.

He trusted that people came in order to learn and grow, and when it was hard, that was all right by him. He didn't care if people had a hard time. He would go up to them when they were having a hard time and he'd say, 'Are you angry? Whose fault is that, mine or yours?' So one really had to give up a lot, but it wasn't to him or for him – it was for oneself. With surrender and dignity one learned to open up and see clearly. It is essential in our practice to be unflinchingly honest about ourselves and the world – just as he was.

He would sit under his *kuṭī*, and various lay visitors and other disciples would come, and also some of his monks would be sitting around, and he would make fun of people. He'd say, 'I'd like to introduce you to my monks. This one, he likes to sleep a lot. And this one, he is always sick, his health is his thing; he just spends his time worrying about his health. And this one is a big eater – he eats more than two or three other monks. And this is a doubter over there, he really likes to doubt, really gets into it. And can you imagine, he had three different wives at the same time. And this one likes to sit a lot, all he does is go and sit in his *kuṭī*; I think he is afraid of people.' And then he'd point to himself and say, 'Myself, I like to play teacher.'

Once, when he came to the USA, there was a man who had been a monk with him for a long time who had then disrobed and taken ordination as a Zen priest. So he said, 'I can't figure out this guy', (this man was acting as his translator), 'he is not quite a monk and he is not quite a lay person. He must be some kind of a transvestite.' And throughout the next ten days he kept introducing this man as Miss whatever his name was – Frank or John: 'This is Miss John. I'd like you to meet my transvestite translator. He can't quite make up his mind.' He was very funny, but he was unstintingly honest. He really could make people look at themselves and their attachments. When I was translating for him, he said, 'Even though I don't speak any English, I know the truth is that my translator leaves out all the really hard things I say. I tell you painful things and he leaves out all the things that have a sting in them, makes them soft and gentle for you. You can't trust him.'

First come dignity and surrender – really seeing the power of one's willingness to live in a full way in the Dhamma. And secondly, one has to learn to see honestly, to be honest about oneself and the people around one, to see one's limits and not to be caught in the things outside. When I asked what is the biggest problem with new disciples, he said, 'Views and opinions about everything. They are all so educated. They think they know so much. When they come to me, how can they learn anything? Wisdom is for you to watch and develop. Take from the teacher what's good, but be aware of your own practice. If I am resting while you all sit up, does it make you angry? If I say that the sky is red instead of blue, don't follow me blindly. One of my teachers ate very fast and made noises as he ate. Yet he told us to eat slowly and mindfully. I used to watch him and got very upset. I suffered, but he didn't. I watched the outside. Later, I learned. Some people drive very fast but carefully, and others drive slowly and have many accidents. Don't cling to rules or to form. If you watch others at the most ten percent of the time and yourself ninety percent, this is proper practice. First I used to watch my teacher, Ajahn Tongrat, and had many doubts. People even thought he was mad. He would do strange things and be very fierce with his disciples. Outside he was angry, but inside there was nobody, nothing there. He was remarkable. He stayed clear and mindful until the moment he died. Looking outside of yourself is comparing, discriminating; you won't find happiness that way. No way will you find peace if you spend your time looking for the perfect man, or the perfect woman or the perfect teacher.'

The Buddha taught us to look at the Dhamma, the Truth, not to look at other people, to see clearly and to see into ourselves; to know our limits. Ram Dass asked him about limits. He asked, 'Can you teach if your own work isn't completed, if you're not fully enlightened?' And he replied, 'Be honest with them. Tell them what you know from your heart and tell people what's possible. Don't pretend to be able to lift big rocks when you can only lift small ones. Yet it doesn't hurt to tell people that if you exercise and if you work, it's possible to lift this. Just be straightforward and assess what's truly reasonable.' Surrender, and dignity in that, and real impeccability: this is the ground. Then there's clarity, seeing what's true in oneself, seeing one's limits, seeing one's attachments.

Then the third way he taught was by working with things.

Working is done in two parts: one by overcoming obstacles and hindrances, and the other by letting go. Overcoming: the first Dhamma talk I gave was at a large gathering, *Māgha Pūjā* festival day, and in a hall filled with 500 or 1,000 villagers. We sat up all night, alternately sitting for one hour and then listening to a talk given by one of the teachers from his monasteries. He had several hundred monks there at that time; they all came together from the branch monasteries for that day. And then in the middle of the night with no preparation, he said, 'Now we'll hear a Dhamma talk from the Western monk.' I'd never given a Dhamma talk before, much less in Lao, the local dialect. There was no time, I had to just get up and say what I could say. He had his chief Western disciple, Ajahn Sumedho, get up and give a talk. Ajahn Sumedho ended after an hour and Ajahn Chah said, 'Talk more.' So Ajahn Sumedho talked another half-hour; he didn't have much to say, people were getting bored, he was getting bored, he finished. Ajahn Chah said, 'Now more.' Another half-hour, three-quarters of an hour, it was getting more and more boring – he'd run out of things to say. People were sleeping; Ajahn Sumedho didn't know what to say, finally finished, and Ajahn Chah said, 'More, a bit more.' Another half-hour – it was the most boring talk! And why would he do it? He got Ajahn Sumedho to learn not to be afraid of being boring. It was wonderful.

He encouraged people to put themselves in situations where they were afraid. He would send people who were afraid of ghosts to sit outside at night in the charnel-ground. I would go sometimes – because I wasn't afraid of ghosts, it was a way of showing off – but for them it was really scary. Or he had people go away out in the forest and meditate, and face the fear of tigers. The spirit of the practice was to really make yourself work with things to overcome them. He pushed you into what you disliked. If you liked to be alone in the forest, you were assigned to a city monastery in Bangkok. And if you liked the city and the easy life and good food, he'd send you to some impoverished forest monastery where there were just rice and tree leaves to eat. He was a real rascal. He knew all of your trips, and he could find them and he would somehow, in a very funny and gentle and yet direct way, really make you look to see where you were afraid or attached. Fear, boredom, restlessness – fine, sit with it. Be bored, be restless and die, he would say over and over again. Die in that restlessness, die in that fear, die in that boredom. People were sleepy, great: the ascetic practice he'd assign would be to sit up all night, and if you wouldn't sit, walk, walk more, walk backwards if you were really sleepy. Whatever it took, to really go against it.

With anger, restlessness, the same. He said, 'You are restless. Fine, go back and sit. Sit more when you are restless, don't sit less.' He said it's like starving a tiger to death in a cage of mindfulness. It's not that you need to do anything about the tiger – the tiger being your anger or restlessness – just let it roam around in the cage. But you make the cage around it with your sitting. He really made people look at where they were, made them face it. But still, it was done with humour and it was done with balance. He wouldn't allow people to do fasts, except very rarely. He wouldn't even allow people to do long solitary practice, unless he felt it was really good for them. Some people he'd make work. 'You need to know the strength of the ox-cart', he would say, 'and not overload it.' He made space for each person to grow at their own pace. The first part of working was really working to overcome difficulties. He said, 'The way of Dhamma is the way of opposites. If you like it cold you should have it hot, and if you like it soft, take it hard.' Whatever it was, to be really willing to let go, to be free.

The second part of working was by the practice of real mindfulness, of being aware of things and letting go of them. In terms of form, this meant to let go of attachments to physical possessions. 'Letting go', however, also included matters of custom. I remember the villagers came to complain to him because he'd set up what still exists as a monastery for training Westerners, and these Westerners were celebrating

Christmas, with a Christmas tree and all. The villagers came and said, 'Listen, you told us we were going to have a forest monastery for Buddhist monks by our village, and these Westerners are doing Christmas. It doesn't seem right.' So he listened to them and said, 'Well, my understanding is that the teachings of Christianity are the teachings of loving-kindness, of surrender and compassion, of seeing one's neighbour as oneself, of sacrifice, of non-attachment – many of the basic principles of Buddha-Dhamma. For me, it seems all right that they celebrate Christmas, especially since it is a holiday of giving and generosity, of love. But if you insist, we won't celebrate Christmas there any more.' The villagers were relieved. He said, 'We'll have a celebration, but instead let's call it ChrisBuddhamas.' And that was the celebration. They were satisfied, and he was satisfied.

It wasn't as if the way to do it was through some particular form, but to let go of form, to let go of doubt. He said, 'You have to learn to watch doubts as they arise. Doubting is natural; we all start off with doubts. What's important is that you don't identify with them or get caught up in endless circles. Instead, simply watch the whole process of doubting. See how doubts come and go. Then you will no longer be victimized by them.' To see them, to know them, to let go. The same with judgement and fear – to feel them, to experience them as physical events, as mental states and yet not be caught. To eventually come to see all of the energies – the difficult ones of anger, fear, sleepiness, doubt and restlessness; the subtle ones of our attachment to pride or to stillness, quietness or even insight. Just to see them and allow them to come and go, and come to a really profound kind of equanimity.

He said, 'Sitting for hours on end is not necessary. Some people think that the longer you can sit, the wiser you must be. I've seen chickens sitting on their nests for days on end. Wisdom comes from being mindful in all postures. Your practice should begin as you wake up in the morning and should continue until you fall asleep. Each person has their own natural pace. Some of you may die at age 50, some at age 65, some at age 90. So too, your practice will not be identical. Don't worry about this. What is important is only that you keep watchful, whether you are working, sitting or going to the bathroom. Try and be mindful and let things take their natural course. Then your mind will become quieter and quieter in any surroundings. It will become still, like a clear forest pool. Then all kinds of wonderful and rare animals will come to drink at the pool. You will see clearly the nature of all things in the world. You'll see many wonderful and strange things come and go, but you will be still. This is the happiness and understanding of the Buddha.'

10

LUANG POR CHAH'S RELICS

Issue 28, published in April 1994.

In January 1994 Ajahn Sumedho and Ajahn Attapemo went to Wat Pah Pong in Thailand and took part in the final ceremonies to enshrine the Atthi-dhātu (relics) of Luang Por Chah. Ajahn Attapemo explains:

It was all done quite beautifully, stretching over seven days. Each day there were periods of meditation and Dhamma talks. On the fourth day, quietly, the abbots from most of the 152 branch monasteries gathered to take the majority of the relics up to the *chedi* (Thai for stūpa, or pagoda) built for the cremation last year. A chamber had been made inside, into which three reliquaries were placed. To add to the blessing, gold necklaces, bracelets and rings were draped over the reliquaries. Some ladies even took their rings off their fingers to be enshrined for posterity. Later that day this chamber was sealed with a concrete lid and granite cap-stone. More than 30,000 people had gathered for the occasion. The final ceremony took place on 16th January, exactly two years after Luang Por Chah's death.

His Majesty King Bhumiphol sent his Chief Privy Officer to lead the ceremony, and sent a royal invitation to Somdet Buddhajahn to give a *desanā*. A bronze and glass stūpa nine feet high had been made for the relics, and the Chief Privy Officer took a crystal platter with thirty selected pieces of the relics and placed this inside the glass section of the stūpa. Somdet Buddhajahn and twenty other important monks invited to honour the occasion led the chanting of 'Jayanto', along with 1,200 more monks sitting inside and around the *chedi*.

Along with the relics were the ashes. These were equally divided among the 152 branch monasteries, including a small packet for every monk and nun.

Also on that day, Ajahn Liem was officially appointed as Abbot of Wat Pah Pong.

11

RECOLLECTIONS BY GREG KLEIN

Issue 29, published in July 1994.

Greg Klein (Ajahn Ānando) 3rd November 1946 - 11th May 1994. Below, Ajahn Sucitto remembers Greg Klein, whose ashes were interred at Cittaviveka on 17th July, when a plaque he had had made was also laid.

Something he wrote about his time helping to nurse Luang Por Chah in his terminal illness not only reflects his own interests, but sums up the life mystery well. 'I like the early morning, the night shift as they call it, very much, because one can spend time alone with Luang Por. From 2 a.m. until maybe 5 a.m. is the time when he seems to sleep the most peacefully. Then a rather busy time follows; depending on what day of the week it is we might clean part of the room, very quietly, and then prepare things for waking him at 5.30 to bathe and exercise him. Then, the weather and his strength permitting, we put him in the chair, the one that was sent from England with the money offered by people in the West. It's a really superlative chair, it does everything except put itself away at night! I had a look at what they had made for Luang Por before. It was quite good for the materials they had, but the wheelchair that he has now is in a class by itself. A sense of great respect and affectionate caring goes into the nursing. Although he has been bedridden for almost six years, he has no bedsores. The monks commented that visiting doctors and nurses are quite amazed at the good condition of his skin. The monks who are nursing him never eat or drink anything or sleep in the room. There is very little talking; usually you only talk about the next thing you have to do for his care. If you do talk, you talk in a quiet manner.

So it is not just a room we nurse him in, it is actually a temple. One of the senior Thai Ajahns asked me how I was feeling about being with Luang Por. First I expressed my gratitude for the opportunity. He said, 'But how are you feeling?' I said, 'Sometimes I feel very joyful, and sometimes not so joyful.' I realized that this was going to be a Dhamma discussion. He was using the opportunity to teach me something. He went on to say that there is a lot of misunderstanding about what is happening to Luang Por. 'Actually, it's just the *saṅkhāras*, the aggregates, going through a certain process.' He said, 'All we really need to do is just let it go, let it cease; but if you did that people would criticize, they would misunderstand and think you were heartless and cruel, and that you would let him die. So because of that, we nurse him, which is fine also.' He then went on to say that the reason we perceive things the way we do is that we are still attached to our views and our opinions. But they are not right, they still have the stench of self. He said that Luang Por practised *mettā bhāvanā*, meditation on loving-kindness, very much, and this is why people were drawn to him; but that has a certain responsibility. 'For myself,' he said, 'I incline quite naturally towards equanimity, serenity. There is no responsibility there, it's light.'

On the last morning, when I arrived at Luang Por's *kuṭī*, he was lying on his side, and I just spent a long time sitting facing him, very consciously directing thoughts of loving-kindness and gratitude towards him, expressing my happiness at having had the great blessing of spending some time with him, of having heard his teaching, appreciated it and incorporated it into my life. The morning went by very easily and rapidly. I was sitting looking at him comfortably asleep, and considering how best to use this very special time. And the message was: see it all as *anicca, dukkha, anattā* – something impermanent, imperfect and impersonal. That's what takes one beyond; it's all right.

12

TIMELESS TEACHINGS

Issue 39, published in January 1997.

These Dhamma reflections were published to commemorate the fifth anniversary of Luang Por Chah's death. They come from a collection of his teachings assembled by Paul Breiter during the 70's. They are presented as an expression of reverence and gratitude.

Everyone knows suffering – but they don't really understand suffering. If we really understood suffering, then that would be the end of our suffering.

Westerners are generally in a hurry, so they have greater extremes of happiness and suffering. The fact that they have many *kilesas* (defilements) can be a source of wisdom later on.

To live the lay life and practise Dhamma, one must be in the world but remain above it. *Sīla*, beginning with the basic five precepts, is the all-important parent of all good things. It is for removing all wrong from the mind, removing that which causes distress and agitation. When these basic things are gone, the mind will always be in a state of *samādhi*. At first, the basic thing is to make *sīla* really firm. Practise formal meditation when there is the opportunity. Sometimes it will be good, sometimes not. Don't worry about it, just continue. If doubts arise, just realize that they, like everything else in the mind, are impermanent.

From this base *samādhi* will come, but not yet wisdom. One must watch the mind at work – see like and dislike arising from sense contact, and not attach to them. Don't be anxious for results or quick progress. An infant crawls at first, then learns to walk, then to run, and when it is full grown, can travel half-way round the world to Thailand.

Dāna (generosity), if given with good intention, can bring happiness to oneself and others. But until *sīla* is complete giving is not pure, because we may steal from one person and give to another.

Seeking pleasure and having fun is never-ending, one is never satisfied. It's like a water jar with a hole in it. We try to fill it but the water is continually leaking out. The peace of the religious life has a definite end, it puts a stop to the cycle of endless seeking. It's like plugging up the hole in the water jar!

Living in the world, practising meditation, others will look at you like a gong which isn't struck, not producing any sound. They will consider you useless, mad, defeated; but actually it is just the opposite.

As for myself, I never questioned the teachers very much, I have always been a listener. I would listen to what they had to say, whether it was right or wrong did not matter; then I would just practise. The same as you who practise here. You should not have all that many questions. If one has constant mindfulness, then one can examine one's own mental states – we don't need anyone else to examine our moods.

Once when I was staying with an Ajahn, I had to sew myself a robe. In those days there weren't any sewing machines, one had to sew by hand and it was a very trying experience. The cloth was very thick and the needles were dull; one kept stabbing oneself with the needle, one's hands became very sore and blood kept dripping on the cloth. Because the task was so difficult I was anxious to get it done. I became so absorbed in the work that I didn't even notice I was sitting in the scorching sun, dripping with sweat.

The Ajahn came over to me and asked why I was sitting in the sun and not in the cool shade. I told him that I was really anxious to get the work done. 'Where are you rushing off to?' he asked. 'I want to get this job done so that I can do my sitting and walking meditation,' I told him. 'When is our work ever finished?' he asked. Oh ...! This finally brought me around.

'Our worldly work is never finished,' he explained. 'You should use such occasions as this as exercises in mindfulness, and then when you have worked long enough, just stop. Put it aside and continue your sitting and walking practice.'

Now I began to understand his teaching. Previously, when I sewed, my mind also sewed, and even when I put the sewing away my mind still kept on sewing. When I understood the Ajahn's teaching I could really put the sewing away. When I sewed, my mind sewed; then when I put the sewing down, my mind put the sewing down also. When I stopped sewing, my mind also stopped sewing.

Know the good and the bad in travelling or in living in one place. You don't find peace on a hill or in a cave; you can travel to the place of the Buddha's enlightenment without coming any closer to enlightenment. The important thing is to be aware of yourself, wherever you are, whatever you're doing. *Viriya*, effort, is not a question of what you do outwardly, but just the constant inner awareness and restraint.

It is important not to watch others and find fault with them. If they behave wrongly, there is no need to make yourself suffer. If you point out to them what is correct and they don't practise accordingly, leave it at that. When the Buddha studied with various teachers, he realized that their ways were lacking but he didn't disparage them. He studied with humility and respect for the teachers, he practised earnestly and realized their systems were not complete, but as he had not yet become enlightened, he did not criticize or attempt to teach them. After he found enlightenment, he recalled those he had studied and practised with and wanted to share his new-found knowledge with them.

We practise to be free of suffering, but to be free of suffering does not mean just to have everything as you would like it, have everyone behave as you would like them to, speaking only that which pleases you. Don't believe your own thinking on these matters. Generally, the truth is one thing, our thinking is another thing. We should have wisdom in excess of thinking, then there is no problem. When thinking exceeds wisdom, we are in trouble.

Taṇhā (desire) in practice can be friend or foe. At first it spurs us to come and practise – we want to change things, to end suffering. But if we are always desiring something that hasn't yet arisen, if we want things to be other than they are, then this just causes more suffering.

Sometimes we want to force the mind to be quiet, but this effort just makes it all the more disturbed. Then we stop pushing and *samādhi* arises. And then in the state of calm and quiet we begin to wonder, 'What's going on? What's the point of it?' ... and we're back to agitation again!

The day before the first *Sanghāyanā*, one of the Buddha's disciples went to tell the Venerable Ānanda: 'Tomorrow is the Sangha council, only *arahants* may attend.' Venerable Ānanda was at this time still unenlightened. So he determined, 'Tonight I will do it.' He practised strenuously all night, seeking to become enlightened. But he just made himself tired. So he decided to let go, to rest a bit as he wasn't getting anywhere for all his efforts. Having let go, as soon as he lay down and his head hit the pillow, he became enlightened.

External conditions don't make you suffer, suffering arises from wrong understanding. Feelings of pleasure and pain, like and dislike, arise from sense-contact – you must catch them as they arise, not follow them, not give rise to craving and attachment, which in turn cause mental birth and becoming. If you hear people talking it may stir you up – you think it destroys your calm, your meditation; but you hear a bird chirping and you don't think anything of it, you just let it go as sound, not giving it any meaning or value.

You shouldn't hurry or rush your practice, but must think in terms of a long time. Right now we have 'new' meditation; if we have 'old' meditation, then we can practise in every situation, whether chanting, working, or sitting in out huts. We don't have to go seeking for special places to practise. Wanting to practise alone is half right, but also half wrong. It isn't that I don't favour a lot of formal meditation (samādhi), but one must know when to come out of it – after seven days, two weeks, one month, two months – and then return to relating to people and situations again. This is where wisdom is gained; too much samādhi practice has no advantage other than that one may become mad. Many monks wanting to be alone have gone off and just died alone!

Having the view that formal practice is the complete and only way to practise, disregarding one's normal life situation, is called being intoxicated with meditation.

Meditation is giving rise to wisdom in the mind. This we can do anywhere, any time and in any posture.

13

AJAHN CHAH'S BIRTHDAY

Issue 46, published in October 1998.

> *Ajahn Viradhammo, who was visiting Thailand, passed on a*
> *letter that he had written to the New Zealand Sangha about*
> *the celebration of Ajahn Chah's birthday at Wat Pah Pong*
> *some time before Luang Por passed away.*

The birthday celebrations at Wat Nong Pah Pong were a magnificent tribute to Luang Por. There were over 600 *bhikkhus* and *sāmaṇeras*, and a sea of white-robed nuns and laypeople around his *kuṭī* on the afternoon of the 16th. Thānavaro, you will remember where you sat when Luang Por was brought outside in his wheelchair. That grassy area was almost entirely filled with the ochre robe.

We bowed in unison and then Ajahn Mahā Amon led the chanting, '*Mahā There pamādena ...*' To my surprise Luang Por's voice answered back (they played a tape over the public address system) '*Yathā vārivahā ...*' Luang Por continued to sit in his chair (he has no choice), and although I couldn't see his face clearly I'm sure he put tremendous effort forth to acknowledge our devotion and gratitude. All of this was of course very moving.

After some time we once again bowed in unison and Luang Por was taken back to his bed for the past six years. In the evening we had chanting and discourses through the night. The *sāla* was overflowing with laypeople and *bhikkhus*, with many sitting outside. The north-east of Thailand is a very special place where so many people still practise and live their religion with tremendous devotion and sincerity.

After midnight it started to rain and by dawn there was water all around (it has been an exceptionally wet year). In the morning before *piṇḍapat* there was a *dāna* offering of bowls, *glots*, mosquito netting and white cloth to all of the senior monks of over eighty branch monasteries. Just to make sure that there were enough sets of requisites, the laypeople from Bangkok put together 108 sets. The abundance and volume of Buddhist devotion and generosity are astounding.

After this *Mahā Sangha* offering we had a *piṇḍapat* around Luang Por's museum. The line of *bhikkhus* stretched from the old *sāla* to the museum. There was mud everywhere and a seemingly endless circle of laypeople offering rice into our bowls. When the meal finally got under way there were six lines of monks and novices outside the length of the eating hall, and a crammed two lines inside. After the meal there were a few more formalities, parting words, and soon all the visitors began to return to their respective monasteries all over Thailand. This tribute was over and I wished you could both have been here with me.

Luang Por's condition is uncertain, although most people say he is weaker. The most notable difference from last year is in his eyes. The pupils are rolled upwards and there is no longer any attention in his eyes. One of the nursing monks said that sometimes he does focus his eyes and look at what is around him, but this is more and more rare. Whatever his physical condition, the power of his practice and teaching is unmistakable. Equally impressive is the continuing dedication people have to his way. There is much work to be done, and Luang Por's impeccability forces one's attention inwards to the source of both freedom and suffering.

14

SOME FINAL WORDS

Issue 67, published in January 2004.

Extract from a talk given by Luang Por Chah to a large gathering of monks and laypeople at Wat Nong Pah Pong, recently translated by Paul Breiter.

In every home and every community, whether we live in the city, the countryside, the forests or the mountains, we are the same in experiencing happiness and suffering; but very many of us lack a place of refuge, a field or garden where we can cultivate positive qualities of heart. We don't have clear understanding of what this life is about and what we ought to be doing. From childhood and youth until adulthood, we learn to seek enjoyment and take delight in the pleasures of the senses, and we never think that danger will threaten us as we go about our lives, forming a family and so on.

There is also for many of us an inner lack of virtue and Dhamma in our lives, through not listening to the teachings and not practising Dhamma. As a result there is little wisdom in our lives, and everything regresses and degenerates. The Buddha, our Supreme Teacher, had loving-kindness (*mettā*) for beings. He led sons and daughters of good family to ordain, practise and realize the truth. He taught them to establish and spread the teaching, and to show people how to live with happiness in their daily lives. He taught the proper ways to earn a livelihood, to be moderate and thrifty in managing finances and to act without carelessness in all affairs.

The Lord Buddha taught that no matter how poor we may be, we should not let it impoverish our hearts and starve our wisdom. Even if there are floods inundating our fields, our villages and our homes to the point where it is beyond our capability to save anything, the Buddha taught us not to let the floods overcome our hearts. Flooding the heart means that we lose sight of and have no knowledge of Dhamma.

Even if water floods our fields again and again over the years, or even if fire burns down our homes, we will still have our minds. If our minds have virtue and Dhamma, we can then use our wisdom to help us make a living and support ourselves. We can acquire land again and make a new start.

I really believe that if you listen to the Dhamma, contemplating it and understanding it, you can make an end of your suffering. You will know what is right to do, what you need to do, what you need to use and what you need to spend. You can live your life according to moral precepts and Dhamma, applying wisdom to worldly matters. Unfortunately, most of us are far from that.

We should remember that when the Buddha taught Dhamma and set out the way of practice, he wasn't trying to make our lives difficult. He wanted us to improve, to become better and more skilful. It's just that we don't listen. This is pretty bad. It's like a little child who doesn't want to take a bath in the middle of winter because it's too cold. He starts to stink so much that the parents can't even sleep at night, so they grab hold of him and give him a bath. That makes him mad, and he cries and curses his father and mother. The parents and the child see the situation differently. For the child, it's too uncomfortable to take a bath in the winter. For the parents, the child's smell is unbearable. The two views can't be reconciled.

The Buddha didn't simply want to leave us as we are. He wanted us to be diligent and work hard in ways that are good and beneficial, and to be enthusiastic about the right path. Instead of being lazy, we have to make efforts.

His teaching is not something that will make us foolish or useless. It teaches us how to develop and apply wisdom to whatever we are doing: working, farming, raising a family and managing our finances. If we live in the world, we have to pay attention and know the ways of the world, otherwise we end up in dire straits. When we have our means of livelihood, our homes and possessions, our minds can be comfortable and upright, and we can have the energy of spirit to help and assist each other. If someone is able to share food and clothing and provide shelter to those in need, that is an act of loving-kindness. The way I see it, giving things in a spirit of loving-kindness is far better than selling them to make a profit. Those who have *mettā* don't wish for anything for themselves. They only wish for others to live in happiness.

When we live according to Dhamma, we feel no distress when looking back on what we have done. We are only creating good *kamma*. If we are creating bad *kamma*, then the result later on will be misery. So we need to listen and contemplate, and we need to figure out where difficulties come from. Have you ever carried things to the fields on a pole over your shoulders? When the load is too heavy in front, isn't that uncomfortable to carry? When it's too heavy behind, isn't that uncomfortable to carry? Which way is balanced and which way is unbalanced? When you're doing it well, you can see it. Dhamma is like that. There is cause and effect – it is common sense. When the load is balanced it's easier to carry. With an attitude of moderation our family relations and our work will be smoother. Even if you aren't rich, you will still have ease of mind; you won't need to suffer over them.

As we haven't died yet, now is the time to talk about these things. If you don't hear Dhamma when you are a human being, there won't be any other chance. Do you think animals can be taught Dhamma? Animal life is a lot harder than ours, being born as a toad or a frog, a pig or a dog, a cobra or a viper, a squirrel or a rabbit. When people see them they only think about killing or beating them, or catching or raising them for food. So we have this opportunity only as humans. As we're still alive, now is the time to look into this and mend our ways. If things are difficult, try to bear with the difficulty for the time being and live in the right way, until one day you can do it. This is the way to practise Dhamma.

So I am reminding you all of the need to have a good mind and live your lives in an ethical way. However you may have been doing things up to now, you should take a look and examine to see whether what you are doing is good or not. If you've been following wrong ways, give them up. Give up wrong livelihood. Earn your living in a good and decent way that doesn't harm others and doesn't harm yourself or society. When you practise right livelihood, then you will live with a comfortable mind.

We should use our time to create benefit right now, in the present. This was the Buddha's intention: benefit in this life, benefit in future lives. In this life, we need to apply ourselves from childhood to study, to learn at least enough to be able to earn a living, so that we can support ourselves and eventually establish a family and not live in poverty. But we sometimes lack this responsible attitude. We seek enjoyment instead. Wherever there's a festival, a play or a concert, we're on our way there, even when it's getting near harvest time. The old folks will drag the grandchildren along to hear the famous singer. 'Where are you off to, Grandmother?' 'I'm taking the kids to hear the concert!' I don't know if Grandma is taking the kids or the kids are taking her. It doesn't seem to matter how long or difficult a trip it might be, they go again and again. They say they're taking the grandchildren, but the truth is that they just want to go themselves. To them, that's what a good time is. If you invite them to the monastery to listen to Dhamma, to learn about right and wrong, they'll say, 'You go ahead. I want to stay home and rest... I've got a bad headache... my back hurts... my knees are sore... I really don't feel well....' But if it's a popular singer or an exciting play, they'll hurry to round up the kids. Nothing bothers them then. That's how some folk are. They make such efforts, yet all they do is bring suffering and difficulty on themselves. They seek out darkness, confusion, and intoxication on the path of delusion.

The Buddha teaches us to create benefit for ourselves in this life, ultimate benefit, spiritual welfare. We should do it now, in this very life. We should seek out the knowledge that helps us do it, so that we can live our lives well, making good use of our resources, working with diligence in ways of right livelihood.

The Buddha taught us to meditate. In meditation we must practise *samādhi*, which means making the mind still and peaceful. It's like water in a basin. If we keep putting things in it and stirring it up, it will always be murky. If the mind is always allowed to be thinking and worrying over things, we will never see anything clearly. If we let the water in the basin settle and become still, then we will see all sorts of things reflected in it. When the mind is settled and still, wisdom will be able to see things. The illuminating light of wisdom surpasses any other kind of light.

When training the mind in *samādhi*, we initially get the idea it will be easy. But when we sit, our legs hurt, our back hurts, we feel tired, we get hot and itchy. Then we start to feel discouraged, thinking that *samādhi* is as far away from us as the sky from the earth. We don't know what to do and become overwhelmed by the difficulties. But if we receive some training, it will get easier little by little.

It's like a city person looking for mushrooms. He asks, 'Where do mushrooms come from?' Someone tells him, 'They grow in the earth.' So he picks up a basket and goes walking into the countryside, expecting the mushrooms to be lined up along the side of the road for him. But he walks and walks, climbing hills and trekking through fields, without seeing any mushrooms. A village person who has gone picking mushrooms before would know where to look for them; he would know which part of which forest to go to. But the city person has had only the experience of seeing mushrooms on his plate. He heard they grow in the earth and got the idea that they would be easy to find, but it didn't work out that way.

Likewise, you who come here to practise *samādhi* might feel it's difficult. I had my troubles with it too. I trained with an Ajahn, and when we were sitting I'd open my eyes to look: 'Oh! Is Ajahn ready to stop yet?' I'd close my eyes again and try to bear it a little longer. I felt it was going to kill me. I kept opening my eyes, but the Ajahn looked so comfortable sitting there. One hour, two hours; I would be in agony, but the Ajahn didn't move. So after a while I got to fear the sittings. When it was time to practise *samādhi*, I'd feel afraid.

When we are new to it, training in *samādhi* is difficult. Anything is difficult when we don't know how to do it. This is our obstacle. But with training, this can change. That which is good can eventually overcome and surpass that which is not good. We tend to become faint-hearted as we struggle – this is a normal reaction, and we all go through it. So it's important to train for some time. It's like making a path through the forest. At first it's rough going, with a lot of obstructions, but by returning to it again and again, we clear the way. After some time, when we have removed the branches and stumps, the ground becomes firm and smooth from being walked on repeatedly. Then we have a good path for walking through the forest. This is what it's like when we train the mind. By keeping at it, the mind becomes illumined.

So the Buddha wanted us to seek Dhamma. This kind of knowledge is what's most important. Any form of knowledge or study that does not accord with the Buddhist way is learning that involves *dukkha*. Our practice of Dhamma should get us beyond suffering; if we can't fully transcend suffering, then we should at least be able to transcend it a little, now, in the present.

When problems come to you, recollect Dhamma. Think of what your spiritual guides have taught you. They have taught you to let go, to give up, to refrain, to put things down; they have taught you to strive and fight in a way that will solve your difficulties. The Dhamma that you come to listen to is for solving problems. The teaching tells you that you can solve the problems of daily life with Dhamma. After all, we have been born as human beings; it should be possible for us to live with happy minds.

15

THIRTY YEARS LATER

Issue 80, published in July 2007.

Questions and answers with Ajahn Sumedho

Q: It's 30 years since you came to England with Luang Por Chah. Why did you leave Thailand?

A: In 1975 the Americans left Vietnam, Laos and Cambodia – French Indochina. Those countries became communist, and there was a 'domino theory' everybody seemed to think would happen: that once those countries fell, the whole of south-east Asia would follow. There was a widespread fear that Thailand would be next. We had established Wat Pah Nanachat for Westerners. I was the head monk and we had about 20 Western monks there at the time, and I remember thinking, 'What's going to happen to us if Thailand goes communist?' So that was the catalyst that started me thinking about the possibilities of establishing a Buddhist monastery elsewhere. I'd never entertained such an idea, never wanted to leave – but because of this notion that Thailand would fall to the communists, this thought came into my mind.

Shortly after that I was invited home because my mother was very ill and they thought she might die, and it seemed to coincide with having that thought. So when I went back to see my mother and father I thought, 'Well, if people are interested maybe we could set something up.' I spent time with my parents in Southern California, and after my mother seemed to get better I went on with Ven. Varapañño (Paul Breiter) to New York and stayed with his parents. I went to Buddhist groups in Massachusetts, where Jack Kornfield and Joseph Goldstein had just opened the Insight Meditation Society. It was clear that was not to be a monastic place. So nothing much happened in the States with respect to people being interested in starting a monastery.

To get back to Thailand I had to go via London, and that's where I met George Sharp. He was the chairman of the English Sangha Trust (EST) and he seemed very interested in me. I stayed at the Hampstead Vihāra, which was closed; he opened it up for me. During the three days I was there he came every evening to talk to me. Then he asked if I would consider living in England, and I said, 'Well, I can't really answer that question, you'll have to ask my teacher, Luang Por Chah, in Thailand.' And this he did; he came a few months later. Luang Por Chah and I were invited to England, and we arrived on 6th May 1977.

Q: And your idea was that if Thailand fell to the communists, this would be a way of preserving this monastic tradition?

A: Yes. And the thing that impressed me was that the English Sangha Trust had already been established 20 years before, in 1956, and though it had tried all kinds of things, it was essentially a trust set up to support Buddhist monks in England – so it was for the Sangha. There was a movement to try to make it more a trust for supporting lay teachers. But George Sharp had this very strong sense that the original purpose of the EST was to encourage Buddhist monks to come and live in England. Several years before he'd met Tan Ajahn Maha Boowa and Ajahn Paññavaddho when they came to visit London. He consulted with them about how to bring good monks to start a proper Sangha presence in England, and Ajahn Maha Boowa recommended they just wait, not do anything and see what happened. So George had closed the Hampstead Vihāra until the right opportunity arose. He wasn't prepared to put just anybody in there. I think he saw me as a potential incumbent. Ajahn Chah was very successful in training Westerners, and in inspiring Western men to become monks. Wat Pah Nanachat was really quite a work of genius at the time. There'd been nothing like it. That was Luang Por Chah's idea.

Q: What did he think about the idea of moving out of Thailand?

A: When I went back to Thailand I told him about it, and of course he never signified one way or the other in situations like that. He seemed interested, but didn't feel a great need to do anything with it. That's why it was important for George Sharp to visit, so that Luang Por Chah could meet him. George was very open to any suggestions that Ajahn Chah had. He had no agenda of his own, but he was interested in supporting Theravādan monks living under the Vinaya system in England. He'd seen so many failures in England over the previous twenty years; there were many good intentions to establish something, but things just seemed to fall apart. They'd send some Englishmen to Thailand for a couple of years to become ordained, and when they came back they'd be thrown straight into a teaching situation or something they weren't prepared for. They had no monastic experience except maybe a short time in a Bangkok temple. So what impressed George was that by that time I'd had quite a few years of training within the monastic system of Thailand and in the Thai Forest tradition, so I wasn't just a neophyte – although in terms of the way we look at things now, when I came to England I had only ten *Vassa*. I don't think any ten-*vassa* monk now would consider doing such an operation! Ajahn Khemadhammo came a couple of weeks before, and then Ajahn Chah and I came together, arriving on 6th May. Later Ajahns Ānando and Viradhammo dropped in, because they had gone to visit their families in North America. During that time I suggested they stay, and Ajahn Chah agreed, so they stayed on with me and there were four of us.

Q: Did Ajahn Chah make a decision at some point, that yes, OK, it would work?

A: Well, when George Sharp came to see him in Thailand Ajahn Chah put him through a kind of test. He was looking at George, trying to figure out what sort of person he was. George had to eat the leftovers at the end of the line, out of old enamel bowls with chips in them and sitting on the cement floor near the dogs. George was a rather sophisticated Londoner, but Ajahn Chah put him in that position and he seemed to accept it. I didn't hear him complain at all. Later on we had meetings, and George made a formal invitation and Luang Por Chah accepted, agreeing that he and I would visit London the next May.

I was curious, because Luang Por Chah was so highly regarded in Thailand that I wondered how he would respond to being in a non-Buddhist country. There's no question of right procedure in Thailand in terms of monastic protocol, but you can't expect that in other countries. What impressed me during the time in England was how Luang Por responded to the situation. Nothing seemed to bother him. He was interested, he was curious. He watched people to see how they did things. He wanted to know why they did it like this or that. He wasn't threatened by anything. He seemed to just flow with the scene and be able to adapt skilfully to a culture and climate he'd never experienced before in his life, living in a country where he couldn't understand what anyone was saying.

He could relate well to English people, even though he couldn't speak a word of English; his natural warmth was enough. He was a very charismatic person in his own right, whether he was in Thailand or in England, and he seemed to have pretty much the same effect on people, whoever they were.

Every morning we went out on alms-round to Hampstead Heath. People would come, Thai people – and Tan Nam and his wife, that's where we met them. They've been supporting us all these years. Generally our reception was excellent. George Sharp's idea was to develop a forest monastery. He felt that the Hampstead Vihāra was a place that could not develop. It was associated with a lot of past failures and disappointment, so his idea was to sell it off in order to find some place in the countryside that would be suitable for a forest monastery. Luang Por Chah said to stay at the Hampstead Vihāra first, to see what would happen. And it was good enough in the beginning. But the aim was always to move out of there, to sell it off and find a forest.

Q: Did you feel confident that it would work? What were your feelings at that time, after Luang Por Chah left?

A: I didn't know what was going to happen, and I wasn't aware of the kinds of problems I was moving into, with the state of the English Sangha Trust. I was quite naïve really. But I appreciated George Sharp's efforts and intentions, and the legal set-up seemed so good: a trust fund that had been established for supporting the Sangha. George seemed to have a vision of this, rather than seeing us as meditation teachers or just using us to spread Buddhism in Europe. I never got that impression from him; in fact he made it very clear that if I just came and practised meditation they'd support that, without even any expectation of teaching. So right from the beginning it was made clear that I wasn't going to be pushed around or propelled by people to fulfil their demands and expectations. It seemed like quite a good place to start outside of Thailand.

But when Luang Por Chah left – he was only there for a month – he made me promise not to come back for five years. He said, 'You can't come back to Thailand for five years.'

Q: So he believed in the project at that point?

A: He seemed to. He was quite supportive in every way. So I said I would do that, and I planned to stay.

George Sharp

I think it was in June 1976 when the phone rang and it was Ajahn Sumedho. He had been given my telephone number by Ajahn Paññavaddho in Thailand, who suggested he should give me a ring if he needed any assistance. Principally he rang to say, 'Could you give me a place that is suitable for me to stay in for a few days?' I said: 'Okay, I'll send a taxi for you', which I did, and he arrived in no time. He was there altogether about three days.

I had work to do, but in the evenings we would talk for hours. He told me something about the tradition. I was very interested, and in the end he said: 'I invite you to come to Thailand and meet my teacher.' I said I would, and in November of that year I got on a plane and went.

I thought Ajahn Chah might agree to having a go at starting a branch in England, and I suspected he had a great deal of confidence in Ajahn Sumedho. In fact, on one occasion when Ajahn Sumedho was translating, I said to Ajahn Chah: 'This is really quite a venture and, quite frankly, Venerable Sumedho is going to have a very tough time at getting this started. Now, I don't know anything about Venerable Sumedho. He comes to me without any reputation whatsoever. But on the other hand, Ajahn Chah, you are a great teacher, you have a considerable reputation and with such a reputation this venture might have a chance of getting off the ground. What can you tell me to give me confidence in the Venerable Sumedho?' Ajahn Sumedho had to translate all this. Ajahn Chah said, 'I don't think he'll get married.' That was terrific, because that is what all the previous *bhikkhus* had been doing at the Hampstead Vihāra.

I came home knowing that Ajahn Chah was coming over and that he was going to bring four *bhikkhus* with him. So what he was effectively doing was bringing a Sangha to England. They were going to have a look at Haverstock Hill, and he was going to make up his mind whether it was worth a go or not. That is more or less what happened. He simply came in and took over the place. In the end he apparently said they were to stay.

Ajahn Sundara

I started cooking at 8 a.m. in the kitchen of the Hampstead Vihāra, to serve the main meal at 10.30. *Anāgārikas* Phil (Ajahn Vajiro) and Jordan (Ajahn Sumano) watched me prepare my favourite dishes and gave me clues on how to go about in a place that was for me still very strange. I was quite intent on my cooking, I wanted it perfect! After presenting the whole meal to the monks, I felt so nervous and self-conscious that I just ran downstairs and left! I had no idea of the Buddhist customs of chanting a blessing, sharing food, etc.

When I first heard Ajahn Sumedho talk about his life as a forest monk in Thailand I was stunned, because for a long time I had imagined a way of life that would include all the qualities he was describing: where intelligence and simplicity, patience and vitality, humour and seriousness, being a fool and being wise, could all happily coexist. During a later conversation he said, 'It is a matter of knowing where the world is, isn't it?' The penny had dropped: 'I am the world!' I had read and heard this truth many times, but I was truly hearing it for the first time. That's when I decided to give monastic life a try, not motivated by the desire to become a nun, but to learn and put into practice the teaching of the Buddha. I had found my path.

Ajahn Vajiro

'Forest *bhikkhus* in London', that's what I heard. I was excited by the news. I bicycled from south of the river, up Haverstock

Hill to number 131, a terraced house opposite the Haverstock Arms. The shrine room on the second floor was as big as could be made from one floor of the house. When Ajahn Chah was there the room was over-full, cramped and stuffy. The talks were long and riveting. Tea was served in the basement afterwards.

I was particularly struck by the way the *bhikkhus* related to each other, and especially how they related to Ajahn Chah. There was a quality of care and attention which I found beautiful. I can remember thinking, 'I'll NEVER bow', and within a few weeks of watching and listening, asking Ajahn Sumedho to teach me how to bow.

When I went to live at the Hampstead Vihāra in early 1978, the place was physically cramped, crowded and chaotic. It was not unusual for six men to be sleeping in the shared *anāgārikas* and laymen's room on the top floor. There were two WC's in the main building, one shower, a tiny kitchen and the small basement room next to the kitchen served as the *dāna sāla*. What kept us there enduring the physical conditions was the quality of the Dhamma. The *pūjās* were early in the morning and included a reflection nearly every day. And with the evening *pūjās*, talks again were almost daily.

The main reflection was on uncertainty. There was a confidence that things would change, and a trust that if the cultivation of *pāramīs* was sincere, the change would be blessed.

Part III

TELEVISION INTERVIEW

16

INTERVIEW WITH AJAHN VAJIRO

Conducted by a French television channel.

Q: *Comment avez-vous découvert cette tradition des moines de la forêt?*

Q: *How did you come across the Forest Monk tradition?*

A: Through an interest in meditation I heard about the Forest Tradition in 1975. In 1977 I heard that there were Forest Monks in London where I was living, so I went to see them. They had been invited to stay in England to live as *bhikkhus*.

Q: *Vous connaissiez bien Ajan Chah, quel souvenir en gardez-vous?*

Q: *You knew Ajahn Chah well. What memories do you have of him?*

A: I cannot claim to have known him well. I did not speak Thai at all then and never lived with him for a long time.

I met him in 1977 during his first trip outside of Thailand. I was struck by how at ease he was in whatever situation he found himself in. In 1979 he travelled outside Thailand again and I was then part of the community. He came to check how the community of four monks he had left in the UK was getting along. At that time someone had offered some woodland for the forest monks, and a derelict house close to that woodland had been bought with the funds from selling the property in London. Ajahn Chah approved of the move, although he could see that the house was not comfortable. He is reported to have often said that to begin a monastery is difficult, but easier than to repair and maintain a monastery, which is more difficult; and finally, that to have good wise monks living in the monastery is the most difficult.

I helped with the driving when he was making a tour of the United Kingdom. We travelled all the way to Edinburgh in a very unsuitable slow van. He never complained or showed any sign of impatience with the van. He did take the opportunity to teach and instruct with economy and humour. I was drying his bowl, and he came over to where I was and with the help of one of the other monks translating explained completely all the stages in taking care of the bowl. And at the end he pointed out, 'I will train you to take care of your bowl, Ajahn Sumedho will teach you to reach Nibbāna.' In this way he was both teaching me and indirectly offering something for Ajahn Sumedho, who was within hearing range, something to learn from.

Later when I was already in Thailand, I awaited the occasion to undertake the full training as a *bhikkhu*. This is called the ceremony of *upasampadā*. By that time in early 1980, I had been both a postulant and a novice for longer than almost any foreign to Thailand person. There were four young novices awaiting the confirmation of the date. But Ajahn Chah would not give us a date. On a number of occasions we would go to his monastery from where we were living, all prepared, all ready, and ask, 'When will the ceremony be arranged?' and he would always just put us off. And then one evening he said, 'Go and prepare the hall, we'll do it tonight.' This was at around five o'clock. So we did, and as the evening fell in the tropics in a monastery without electricity, the ceremony took place. Simple and easy. With no fuss. It happened to be my birthday. To this day I do not know if Ajahn Chah knew or, if he did know, whether he thought it at all important.

Q: Revenons maintenant, si vous voulez bien, sur cette tradition des Moines de la Forêt que vous représentez... Est-ce que vous pouvez nous rappeler quand elle est née, et dans quelles circonstances...?

Q: Please let us come back to this 'Forest Monk' Tradition that you represent. Could you remind us when it was born and in what circumstances?

A: The Forest Monk tradition is not confined to Thailand and would have existed in some form from the time of the Lord Buddha.

Q: Est-ce qu'on peut définir la particularité de cette tradition?

Q: Can we define the specificities of this tradition?

A: The particular branch of the Forest Tradition to which I belong, Wat Pah Pong, is distinguished by its working as a community. It works together. It seems to be Ajahn Chah's great offering, the offering of encouraging people to work together in community. He used the Vinaya, the Training in Community, as received from the traditional scriptures, and worked out how to allow ordinary people to use that training to learn to live and work together.

Often when a great teacher dies the disciples go their own way. You may have heard that Ajahn Chah was paralyzed and did not speak for about the last ten years of his life. This was certainly difficult for all of us, those who called themselves his disciples. The effect was that we all had to learn to work together. There were five people nursing him all the time of his illness. The monks took turns. They had to work together.

Today the group consists of maybe 1,500 monastics, with about 270 monasteries. Of those monastics, about 150 would not call Thailand their origin. There are about 20 monasteries not run by Thais which would look to Wat Pah Pong and that tradition. I think around 17 of those monasteries are not in Thailand.

The monasteries vary in size from maybe two monastics, or even one, to maybe 50. Outside Thailand the largest in number of monastics is probably Amaravati Buddhist Monastery.[1] We all consider ourselves part of this family.

Q: *Le maître a un rôle très important dans cette tradition...*

Q: *The teacher has a very important role in this tradition ...*

A: The teacher has an important role, yes. Like the father.

---

[1] www.forestsangha.org/monasteries

Q: Quelles sont les règles qu'un moine de la forêt doit observer?

Q: What are the rules a forest monk should observe?

A: There are four which if not observed, automatically, with immediate effect and without ceremony, disqualify a man from continuing the training.

1. Any sexual intercourse

2. Theft of something of value

3. Shortening or causing to be shortened the life of any human.

4. Lying deliberately to claim that one has attained some special spiritual level.

The particular rule of our tradition and family, which is common to all Buddhist monks with a connection to the training at the time of the Lord Buddha, is not to own or control personal money or that which counts as money.

Q: Comment la communauté des moines de la forêt s'est-elle créée puis a-t-elle évolué en Angleterre?

Q: How was the Forest Sangha created in England and how did it develop?

A: The Forest Sangha has evolved in the UK through the confidence of and confidence in the disciples of Ajahn Chah, particularly Ajahn Sumedho. He has allowed communities of monastics to grow in the UK. The confidence has been that if the monastics are living in accordance with what can be shown to be the teaching of the Lord Buddha, then there will be enough generosity to support that life. The places where monastics live in community can be like generators: generators of generosity (they exist because those who live there are generous in their lives and what they offer, asking for nothing, and those who support that life are generous in offering that support of material things); generators of virtue (the places encourage virtue in those who live there and, through example and direct teaching, encourage virtue in those who visit); and generators of an attitude which cultivates reflection or wisdom (they are places where people meditate, examine their universe from the inside and practise being enlightened).

Q: *Quelles ont été les principales difficultés?*

Q: *What were the main difficulties?*

A: The principal difficulty is that of attachment to opinions and views, and the pain that follows.

Q: *Vous avez participé, au début des années 80, à l'établissement du monastère d'Amaravati, en Angleterre... le premier monastère de forêt en Occident... Est-ce que cela n'a pas été trop compliqué? Les réactions ont-elles été favorables?*

Q: *You took part at the beginning of the 80's in the establishment of Amaravati, the first forest monastery in the West. Wasn't that too complicated? Was the public response positive?*

A: Amaravati was not the first forest monastery, that was Chithurst Forest Monastery, Cittaviveka.[1]

---

[1] www.cittaviveka.org

Yes, beginning any monastery is difficult. Not much more difficult in the West than in the East. A little different. When something a little out of the ordinary arrives somewhere, there are always a variety of responses. The main concern seemed to be traffic. Would the place attract more cars? There were other worries that the strangeness of the clothing and customs would somehow undermine what was already there. Again a clinging to views and opinions.

Q: *Quelles sont les grandes différences avec la communauté des moines de la forêt en Thaïlande?*

Q: *What are the main differences between the Western Sangha and the Thai one?*

A: The main difference is maybe the timing of the meal. In Thailand it is long established that the meal is around 08.30 to maybe 09.00, and that will be the meal for the day. Outside Thailand the meal is usually a little later, maybe 10, 10.30 or even 11.30. This is because it is thought that this will make it easier for people to come to the monastery to be part of that occasion. Of course there are some differences of dress to accommodate the differences in climate.

Q: *Les échanges, les liens entre les deux communautés sont-ils aussi forts aujourd'hui?*

Q: *Are the links between the two communities still as strong today?*

A: The links nowadays are still strong, almost stronger in the last few years than they were in the early 80's and mid-80's. Communication is now a lot less expensive.

Part IV

A RECENT RECOLLECTION

17

THE LUANG POR CHAH
MEMORIAL WEEK

Recollections by Ajahn Siripañño.

Every year during the week leading up to the anniversary of Ajahn Chah's death on 16th January, there is a great gathering at his monastery in north-east Thailand, when many of his disciples come together for six days of Dhamma practice. Ajahn Siripañño, the senior monk at Wat Dtao Dam at the time of writing, provides the following account from his perspective of living as a monk in Ajahn Chah's branch monasteries in Thailand.

12th January 2009, and all over Thailand motorbikes, cars, pick-up trucks, mini-vans and tour buses are making their way to the north-eastern province of Ubon, heading for a certain monastery – Wat Pah Pong. Those making the journey are looking to spend a week imbibing the spirit and teachings of a forest master now long gone, Ajahn Chah. Most never met him in person, but the books, tapes and first-hand accounts of his life have inspired them enough to make changes in their lives, to take up meditation, and now to join the annual pilgrimage to where it all began and take part in a week of communal Dhamma practice.

The name of the event translates as 'Dhamma practice festival in honour of the Teacher'. Actually, the word *ngan* – here translated as 'festival' – usually means work. But it can also mean any kind of event or celebration: birthdays, weddings, funerals, festivals – any kind of activity, really. The Ajahn Chah *ngan* combines many things: the serious spiritual work of keeping precepts, meditating and listening to Dhamma talks, socializing with old friends, and having fun making new ones.... This is against the backdrop of reaffirming one's dedication to living in line with the teachings of the Lord Buddha and, more recently, Ajahn Chah, or Luang Por ('venerable father') as he is affectionately known. Of the thousands who arrive from near and far, some come to practise and hear the Dhamma, some to give and participate in large measure or small, and some come just to check out the scene, and enjoy the free food available for all.

Luang Por Chah passed away on 16th January 1992, and every year since his funeral on that date the following year, a gathering has taken place at his monastery Wat Pah Pong. The number of participants keeps increasing. This year saw over a thousand monks and novices and five thousand laypeople put up mosquito nets (and, more and more these days, tents) all over the monastery, doing their best to let go of the outside world and focus their hearts on a different dimension. With Luang Por's teachings as the conduit, the practice turns one inwards – to taste peace, know truth and find oneself.

Tan Ajahn Liem, the abbot of Wat Pah Pong (and these days himself referred to as 'Luang Por') is sitting under his *kuṭī* receiving some monks as they arrive to pay their respects. A man of few words, he gives the young monks advice and encouragement like a warm father. 'It just got a bit colder, but it's not too bad. Last night was about 15 degrees. It'll take a couple of days for the body to adjust, that's all. If you put your sleeping sheet directly on the hay it will be warmer. A plastic groundsheet will stop your body heat from getting trapped in the hollow stalks, so you'll be colder. We have plenty of toilets these days, so you should be comfortable ... not like before. There's space to put up your mosquito nets behind the Uposatha Hall. Around the *chedi* is full of laypeople these days, so it's not so appropriate. How many of you came? For the next few days you should surrender to the schedule. This will help eradicate unwholesome states of mind such as arrogance and conceit, and the need to have things your own way. Otherwise you will always fall under the sway of defilements and craving. It takes effort, though – *viriyena dukkhamacceti*: "suffering is overcome through effort". But if you practise correctly your hearts will experience the happiness of inner peace.'

He pauses and looks up. 'Have you set up your bowls for the meal yet? No? Off you go then. It's almost time.'

The monks and novices head for the eating hall, directly behind the main *sāla* which is now slowly filling with white-clothed laypeople. Women far outnumber men. Before the meal every day the Eight Precepts are given and there is a half-hour Dhamma talk. On this, the first day, it is Luang Por Liem, like a welcoming host, who gives the introductory talk. He stresses that initially we have come out of faith in the Buddha and Luang Por Chah, but that in order to carry out their teachings we need to develop true *sati* – true mindfulness:

'We are all just part of nature: the body must change and return to its origins. When we think in this way the mind will tend to seclusion, rather than clinging to views and conceit. Dwelling secluded in body and mind, we are able to see the true nature of reality. And so we won't fall under the sway of things that can obsess the mind and wrong views which stain the mind. The body is just a natural resource we can make use of – not a being, not a person, animal or individual. If we understand this the mind will feel cool and happy, not anxious and confused. If we strive in this way we will attain the goal we are seeking. We have a good opportunity, so try to do it: renounce and abandon the things that cause you worry. The Buddha taught us to abandon all worldly dhammas. We can't even depend on our friends and relatives. Ultimately we have to build our own inner refuge.'

He outlines the daily routine, emphasizing the need to be harmonious and helpful as we will be spending a week living together in such large numbers. Meditation, too, is taught in brief.

'Breathe in and out. See that it's just nature doing its job, breath coming in and going out. When we understand that our awareness of this is an aspect of our mind, we see that even this is a *saṅkhata dhamma* (a conditioned phenomenon). There is no self in there. The mind experiences the breath. The mind has no physical matter, yet that is where *dukkha* arises. All mental states are impermanent, so develop the quality of patient endurance with regard to all mental states, good and bad. Usually we get lost in our moods, and this keeps us away from the correct path of practice ...

'Whatever posture you are in, you are grounded on the earth. Keep this deep awareness (Thai: *poo roo*) in mind all the time. This way you won't think of the body as a self. It will lead to a pure happiness arising in the mind. Instead of delighting in those things which deceive us – things people run to like insects drawn to a flame – cultivate faith in the Buddha's awakening ... Develop yourself internally with your mind and externally with your actions. You all know the duties regarding the lodgings and toilets. They are communal property, not owned by anyone, including the abbot. People who are mindful keep a place clean and well maintained.'

Knowing it's almost nine o'clock, he concludes, 'Now it's time to provide our bodies with the sustenance we need to carry us through the next day and night, so I will end there. I wish to express my gladness that you have all come, and encourage you to make a firm determination to practise with integrity this week.'

For the rest of the day, monks and laypeople arrive at Wat Pah Pong in a constant stream. Luang Por Liem receives incoming Sangha members under his *kuṭī* all day, and by evening he still has not had a chance to find his own spot in the forest to put up his mosquito net and lay down a bed of straw like everyone else. He is just slipping away when a monk approaches him quickly to say that Ajahn Sumedho has arrived to pay respects.

He returns to his seat, first putting on his robe, and the large group of Western *bhikkhus*, including Ajahn Sumedho, bows three times. The two old friends chat for a while, inquiring after each other's health, and Luang Por Liem asks about the various branch monasteries in England. They have known each other for almost 40 years. Practising together in the old days, travelling on *tudong* and serving their teacher – theirs is a lifelong bond, bound up with much mutual warmth and respect. All over the monastery similar scenes are taking place: monks who have spent time together in the past are now meeting again, paying respects and catching up, like childhood friends.

After about half an hour there is a pause and Luang Por Liem, a little sheepishly, excuses himself. 'It will be getting dark soon, I still haven't put up my net.' There are smiles all round and the visitors again bow three times. Luang Por Liem disappears into the twilight of the forest.

By the evening of the first day, several hundred monks have arrived and the number of laypeople is over three thousand. There are free food distribution tents set up – over a hundred different stalls and marquees sponsored by individuals, branch monasteries, government offices and other groups. For the next week, almost round the clock there will be all kinds of food and drink available for anyone who wants them. Luang Por Kampan Ṭhitadhammo mentioned this in the talk he gave on 15th January.

'It's as if the whole country is coming together here. This is the result of Luang Por's life. Just look at the food tents. It's like a wholesome cycle of goodness. People come here to hear the Dhamma. Then they give food to others. Other people come to eat, but in doing so they get to listen to the Dhamma. Then they in turn want to give.'

Some locals, unable to sponsor a tent for the whole week, simply drive their pick-up into the monastery with the back full of some kind of tasty snack. Parking it just inside the monastery gate, they hand out their offerings to passers-by. In not too long the food is gone and they drive off, happy to have been a part of the event and to have taken the family on such a fun outing.

The local hospitals provide first-aid tents as well as traditional Thai massage and reflexology for the Sangha members. Last year there was free dental treatment and this year eye tests and glasses were offered in a marquee just opposite Luang Por's *chedi*. Over the years the scope of the gathering has broadened, as well as the range of participants. Lay supporters from Abhayagiri monastery in California won the hearts of everyone when they prepared and served American snacks from a food tent they set up a few years ago. Professionals and teachers from Bangkok come and camp around the *chedi*, as well as members of what the Thais call '*Hi So*' (from the English 'high society') – slang for the aristocracy and well-heeled elite, who genuinely want to put down much of the superficiality and stress of modern life and reconnect with something more meaningful and peaceful. Some tents may be fancier than others, but everyone keeps the Eight Precepts and most stick diligently to the schedule – sharing together in the pre-dawn chill of morning chanting, queuing for food and toilets and splashing down with a bucket of cold water to bathe. It is no small matter for some.

Every year more schoolchildren come in large groups. All wearing white – girls camping in one area, boys in another – they have all the playful energy of teenagers everywhere. But a genuine sense of respect and decorum is also there, as if they know that although it's not as much fun as a usual school trip, somehow it's important, and it's only a few days after all.

It's 2.45 a.m. Way too early. But from the high bell tower to the north of the eating hall, the repetitive striking shatters the stillness. It's time for morning chanting. You do have a choice, though; you could try to find an excuse to stay bundled up in a heap of robes on the cosy bed of straw. You're still a bit weak from that diarrhoea a few days ago, your throat seems to hurt a bit – wouldn't want to get sick on day two – with so many monks, no one else would really notice if you weren't there. But it's useless. Only the previous day, in a talk to the Sangha, Ajahn Anek had reminded everyone that in Luang Por's time everyone was at morning chanting, and not all wrapped up in brown shawls and blankets, either. Then you had to sit with your right shoulder exposed, patiently enduring the cold weather and practising *ānāpānasati* (mindfulness of breathing). You imagine Luang Por Chah's presence standing next to where you are lying curled up, looking down stony-faced: 'Eugh! Is this how you practise?' Spitting out some red betel-nut juice, he turns around and disappears into the void. You don't really have a choice.

By 3.05 the *sāla* is nearly full with monks sitting, as is the eating hall. With the exception of one monk known for his eccentricity who has crafted himself a Mexican-style poncho, almost no *bhikkhus* are wrapped in blankets as they were the previous morning. Ajahn Anek's words have had the desired effect, and the new generation of monks seems keen to show its fighting spirit.

The laypeople, who somehow seem to have more enthusiasm for morning chanting than do the monks, have gathered *en masse*, and the women – *mae awks* as they are known in the local dialect – fill the *sāla* and flow back out along a wide concrete road. At 3.15 the old grandfather clock chimes and one of the senior monks rings a bell: '*Gra-ahp*' he says over the microphone, Thai for 'It's time to bow and chant.' '*Yo so Bhagavā ...*' The monk with the microphone tries to push the pace and raise the pitch, but the massed ranks of *mae awks* have the strength of numbers and the chanting stays slow and low. Some find the whole thing tedious; others are filled with devotion and inspiration. For 45 minutes these ancient Pāli words and their modern Thai translation are recited line by line, to a slightly singsong melody that is written only in the hearts of those who know it and who learned it themselves by listening and following along from the time they first came to the monastery.

From 4 until 4.45 there is a period of meditation. Fighting the cold and fatigue, for many it's nothing but a struggle not to wrap up, fall asleep, or both. Others seem to have found an equanimity of body and mind. Seated on the hard granite floor, they embody the peace and wisdom of the Buddhas; still and silent, aware and knowing, breath going in, breath going out.

By 5 a.m. the monks are setting up the eating hall, sweeping, mopping, and putting out tissues, water and spittoons. Next they prepare their bowls and put on their robes for alms-round. A senior monk has the microphone and is going through some of the points of etiquette for alms-round: wearing one's robes properly, walking with eyes downcast, not swinging the arms and body about, keeping silent, and many other minor points of practice. Some newly ordained monks and novices may still be learning all this. Others will have heard it year in, year out. Yet somehow it has a freshness every time and an immediate relevance. These minor training rules and the small points of monastic etiquette, collectively called *kor wat* in Thai, were given huge importance by Luang Por Chah as the way to begin training the mind: by letting go of doing things one's own way and being mindful to do things the prescribed way. The Buddha laid down these principles over 2,500 years ago, and Luang Por knew their value.

Wat Pah Pong has about a dozen alms routes that wind through the surrounding villages. But when a thousand or so *bhikkhus* are in need of some sustenance, it's the nearby town of Warin and the city of Ubon that provide much of the additionally-required calories. As dawn approaches, the monks head out of the monastery gates, each with an alms bowl and some with two if they are attending a senior *bhikkhu*. Lining the road to the left, right and directly in front of the gate is a motley fleet of assorted vehicles: draughty buses and pick-ups and, for the lucky ones, warm mini-vans. The monks swarm aboard and wait. At an unseen signal, suddenly engines rev and wheels roll, and the parade of vehicles heads for various markets and residential areas. When they arrive at their destination the monks form lines of up to 50 or more and walk along pre-designated routes. People of all ages line the way and make their offerings, doing their bit for the *ngan*. The food is simple but bountiful, and by the end of the alms-round each monk may have emptied his full bowl up to a dozen or more times: sticky rice, boiled eggs, instant noodles, orange drinks, tinned fish, bananas, coconut sweets ... staples of the modern Isan (north-east Thai) diet woven into this hallowed Isan custom – offering food to the monks at dawn. No amount of economic crisis, it seems, can deprive people of this simple joy. And no matter how often one has taken part in this act of giving and receiving, it remains a little mysterious, and quite magical.

The buses and pick-ups return with the monks and countless baskets brimming with food. There are still two hours until the Sangha will eat, and as they walk past the food tents the novices and young monks glance enviously at laypeople nibbling away on breakfast snacks. The more senior monks keep their eyes down, having by now learned that watching someone else eat while you are cold and hungry makes neither you nor the other person feel any better.

Everyone gathers at 8 a.m. in the main *sāla* for the daily taking of the Precepts. A *desanā* then follows, inevitably covering familiar ground: our debt of gratitude to Luang Por; the importance of *sīla* as the basis of happiness and the stepping-stone to *samādhi* and *paññā*; meditation and the need to see through the illusory nature of our thoughts and moods, to go beyond desire by establishing a peaceful mind and taste that special happiness the Buddhas praised and that Luang Por experienced for himself, doing everything he could for us to be able to do so as well.

'Careful not to take too much food; think of all the people still behind you ... A purse has been found with some money and keys. If you think it's yours, come and claim it, but you have to say what colour it is and how much money is in there ... Remember not to store food in your mosquito nets. Ants will come for it – and you'll be tempted to eat after midday....'

After the meal, once the Sangha members have washed and dried their bowls, Luang Por Liem gives a 15 minute exhortation, with speakers hooked up in both the monks' and nuns' eating halls, encouraging us all to reflect on our duties as *samaṇas*, recluses who have gone forth from the household life into homelessness: from cleaning toilets to realizing Nibbāna and everything in between.

By 10.30 the sun is filtering through the tall trees and slowly warming up the forest – time for most people to have a quick lie-down before the 1 p.m. gathering for meditation and more Dhamma instruction. These days the Sangha gathers in the *Uposatha* Hall, or *bot* (a Thai short form of the Pāli word *uposatha*), the building where Sangha rituals such as ordinations take place. The *bot* is jam-packed with monks and the heat and stuffiness build up. Heads begin to nod, then droop entirely. At 2 p.m. a senior monk gives a talk. A frequent refrain in these afternoon talks particularly aimed at the monks is how tough it was living at Wat Pah Pong in the early days. All requisites, including food, were scarce. You couldn't even pick your own food, as it was ladled into your bowl for you. There was rarely a sweet drink in the afternoon, and chores were physically draining, including hauling water from a well to fill jars for toilets, bathing and foot-washing. Then there were sweeping, cleaning and general mainten- ance. If something was broken you tried to fix it, and if it couldn't be repaired you went without. Requesting a new one wasn't an option. But it's the love and respect for Luang Por Chah that come across most vividly from these elder-most senior monks, as expressed in a talk from Ajahn Anek.

'Luang Por wished us well from head to toe. Even if our minds didn't like what he was teaching us, our actions had to comply. We were like children bathing in a cesspit. Our loving father comes along and says, 'Children, what are you doing that for?' 'It's fun.' 'Get out. Now!' And Dad reaches in and pulls us out, and gets water to clean us. And pulling us out is no easy job. Some Ajahns leave their disciples to wallow in the cesspit. But Luang Por never did. With just his instruction he was able to extract poison from our hearts. It was like taking a bitter medicine which tasted awful, but we knew it would save our lives ...

'Luang Por's teaching spread far and wide: Patiently endure. Endure with patience. Dare to be patient. Dare to endure. *Khantī paramaṃ tapo tītikkhā:* patient endurance is the supreme incinerator of defilements. *Khantī,* or patient endurance, is like a fire that no coal or electricity could ever produce. We chant *tapo ca brahmacariyañca* – the austerities of leading the Holy Life. These are the austerities that can burn up our defilements.

'One aspect of this is the morning and evening chanting ... Please give up your own preferences and be present for these activities. If during morning chanting there are no monks, but for the meal there are loads, it feels a bit strange, doesn't it? Between following your own preferences, or the opinion of society, or the Dhamma – which is better? These days notions of personal liberty have so filled people's minds that they have no room for Dhamma any more. Luang Por is still with us in spirit. So I ask everyone to please meet together in harmony, so that if Luang Por were here in person he would be happy.'

The Sangha pays respects to the senior monk who has given the talk and an announcement is made to go to the eating hall for the afternoon drink ... 'if there is one.' It's a slightly tongue-in-cheek reminder that we shouldn't take anything for granted. These days, though, there is always something available. Tea, cocoa, freshly squeezed sugar-cane and orange juice; drinks containing aloe vera chunks and other afternoon-allowable 'medicinal' nibbles: sugarcane lumps, candied ginger and a kind of bitter-sour laxative fruit known as *samor*. The laypeople too have had their fill of afternoon Dhamma, and those keeping the Eight Precepts partake of similar fare.

Everyone is encouraged to take part in a group walking meditation circumambulation around the *chedi*, the monument to Luang Por Chah where his crystallized bones, revered by many as holy relics, are kept. All too soon it is almost 6 p.m. and the bell is ringing for evening chanting. The relentlessness of the schedule is a reflection of Luang Por's training methods: keep everyone pushing against their own preferences and desires in order to go beyond them; surrender to the communal routine and allow the sense of self to dissolve into a group identity; and beyond that to experience the sense of being nothing other than nature arising and passing away; to have constant reminders and teachings so that the Dhamma seeps into one's mind – and the transformation from being one who suffers through clinging to one who is free through letting go can take place.

The first hour of the evening session is silent meditation. The January air is crisp and cool, and it is the mosquitoes' feeding time. The *sāla* is full, and all around it and stretching into the forest are men and women wrapped in white, some young though most older, simply sitting, being aware of the in- and the out-breath. Inside the *chedi* too people are meditating, finding warmth in the enclosed space and inspiration from being so physically close to Luang Por's remains. As they sit, groups of people, families, children, stream in and out and pay respects – three bows – before heading off, perhaps to get some noodles at the food tents, or maybe just going home. Over in the *sāla* the chanting begins, and the voice of the monk leading it drifts into the *chedi* from a nearby loudspeaker. Many of the meditators stay motionless, but most slowly open their eyes, and shift their posture from cross-legged to kneeling in the traditional Thai way for chanting. By some kind of unvoiced mutual consent they agree that the monks' pitch is a little too high and settle for something a few tones lower – creating an eerie discord which echoes hauntingly around the inside of the chamber.

Outside it's noticeably colder. By the time the evening *desanā* starts at around 8 p.m. the northern wind has picked up, adding to the talk the flavour of *khantī* – patient endurance. This was always one of Luang Por's favourite themes anyway, one reflects. The monks giving the week's evening talks are Luang Por Chah's most senior disciples. They know how to inject lightness and humour into their teachings; stories of Luang Por abound, as well as humorous anecdotes from their own lives. The language used is mainly central Thai, but those monks who are native to the north-east will often switch abruptly to the local Isan dialect, a language full of puns, wordplay and innuendo, much to the delight of the local crowd. Dhammapada verses, old sayings, and nearly-forgotten proverbs are given an airing, complete with the Ajahn's personal commentary. Isan is not a written language, and listening to these old monks one gets a sense of the power of an oral tradition. Even if none of Luang Por's teachings had been recorded, we would still be able to enjoy them today from the minds and through the voices of the disciples he touched. The Buddha's teachings were not written down for several centuries, yet they managed to survive in a similar way.

You are asleep the second your head hits the straw mattress. One day merges seamlessly into another – all too soon that monk in the bell tower is doing his thing and you find yourself heading back to the *sāla* for morning chanting. Each day is a little easier, though. The floor seems less hard. It's a bit warmer, too. The mind is uplifted, buoyed by the company of so many people sharing the space and practising in the same way. Surely that's what it is – though maybe it's something else....

16th January

The big day arrives. As if to acknowledge one of the unique
aspects of Luang Por's legacy, the international Sangha, the
morning Dhamma talk will be given by Ajahn Jayasāro, who
is English. The evening programme will feature Dhamma
talks to be given throughout the night, but the first one – the
prime-time slot – will be from Luang Por Sumedho.

It is 17 years to the day since Luang Por passed away.
He was cremated on the same day one year later. The main
event of the day is a mass circumambulation of the *chedi* by
the whole assembly. The numbers will swell to many hundreds more, boosted by people who have come just for this
event. With the whole Sangha and all the laypeople gathered
together like a sea of brown robes followed by a white foamy
wake, the effect is quite magical. Beginning in the main *sāla*,
the assembly walks in complete silence, everyone holding a
small set of candles, flowers and incense, for the few hundred
metres until the *chedi*, which the procession then circumam-
bulates. As everyone gathers round the *chedi*, a senior monk
reads out a dedication to Luang Por and everyone follows,
reciting line by line. The Sangha leads the way up the steps
and into the *chedi*. Each person places their little offering,
then bows and makes way for someone else.

In the evening Luang Por Sumedho begins his *desanā*.
Before moving to loftier dhammas, he too entertains the
crowd with some warm old memories. He recalls how Luang
Por used to teach the Dhamma for hours on end, crack-

ing jokes and telling stories which would have everyone in stitches – except for one person: Venerable Sumedho, this newly arrived American monk squirming in pain on the cement floor, unable to understand a word. They've heard it before, but again it brings smiles. These stories though, are not told just to get a few laughs. They capture the spirit of a bygone era for those of us who never heard Luang Por Chah teach, and they prepare the minds of the listeners to hear and be more likely to truly receive the essence of the Dhamma: that all is uncertain and unstable, and that happiness comes from letting go.

Which is just the insight you need in order to last through a whole night of Dhamma talks. This all-night talks routine seems to be a unique feature of the Wat Pah Pong tradition – and you have to be seriously dedicated to hearing Dhamma to even want, let alone be able, to sit on a hard floor for ten hours. Understanding the language, too, is a distinct advantage. Most people nip off for a small rest at some point in the evening; but some seem to sit motionless throughout, in a kind of '*desanā* trance'. The first couple of speakers talk for about an hour; after that it's half an hour each. So, altogether 15 or so Dhamma talks ring throughout the forest on loudspeakers right through till dawn. A bell is struck to let any speaker who's getting a bit carried away know that his 30 minutes are up. The style of *desanā* is usually unstructured, which is typical of the Thai forest tradition. Anyone who miscalculates his allotted time can therefore easily wrap up and make way for the next speaker when he hears the bell.

The last speaker is still going at full speed at 5 a.m. as the monks, for one last time, begin to set up the eating hall and then stream out through the gates towards the waiting armada of alms-round road transport.

On this last morning the Sangha and laity gather in the *sāla* one final time, to take leave and ask forgiveness of the most senior monks. After a week of remembrance dedicated to Luang Por Chah, it seems fitting that the endnote is an acknowledgement of our present-day teachers. Luang Por Liem, appointed by Luang Por Chah to be his successor as abbot of Wat Pah Pong, receives the traditional offerings of tooth-woods – wooden toothbrushes made from a bitter vine that the monks meticulously fashion in advance and bring to the gathering to give to senior Ajahns as a token of respect.

After a few words of farewell and one last blessing the 2009 memorial gathering is over. The last meal is taken and followed by a mass exodus. Thousands of mosquito nets are taken down and tents dismantled; vans are loaded, with as many as 15 people crammed in to the back of a pick-up truck for journeys of up to several hundred kilometres. Rubbish is collected and areas swept. In the eating hall the spittoons are dried one last time, the water bottles bagged up for recycling, the sitting mats put away. Within a few hours the monastery feels deserted. Only the resident community of 40 or so monks and the nuns in their own section remain, doing the final clear up.

The following day is a Sunday. In the afternoon some visitors, including a couple from Bangkok, stop by Wat Pah Pong to pay respects, and hopefully make some offerings to Luang Por Liem. A lone monk sweeps the concrete road around the *chedi*, and not a trace remains of the thousands of residents over the previous week or the mass circumambulation the day before. Not someone who seems too interested in taking a break after a hard day's night, Luang Por Liem is in town looking for building materials. He won't be long, though, the group is told. Sure enough, within half an hour he is back. 'I went into town to get some pipes. We are building more toilets for next year's gathering. More and more people seem to come. More people means more waste. It's natural. If we can see the body as part of nature – natural elements and not a self – then peace will arise in the heart. This peace leads to true happiness.'

Extracts from a desanā given by Ajahn Jayasāro

It's been 17 years now since Luang Por left us, although actually that is not quite true. Luang Por never left us – we are the ones who leave him behind. Every time we think, say, or do something of which he pointed out the danger, we leave him behind. There are so many of his teachings around: books, tapes etc. His Dhamma is still with us. But we frequently leave his teachings behind, sometimes turning our backs on the Dhamma entirely. Luang Por Chah is not with us today, but the question is, are we still with Luang Por Chah?

... Not having Right Understanding (*sammā diṭṭhi*) is what will prevent true happiness from arising. We won't see the true nature of the world: the fact that *dukkha* is everywhere. The good news is that true happiness can also be found. It is not about suppressing the happiness that we can experience through the eye, ear, nose, tongue, body and mind, but rather asking ourselves if that is true happiness. Is that what we ultimately need ? Sensory happiness makes us waste our time, and diverts our interest away from developing ourselves to find that true happiness.

Say you had enough money to go abroad and you flew to some other country. Then from the airport you went straight to a hotel, checked in and went to your room, closed the windows and stayed there for two weeks. You then went back to the airport and flew home. Would that be unwholesome? No. But it would be a pity, a wasted opportunity. Being born as a human being, but only being interested in the pleasure of sights, sounds, smells, tastes, touch and thoughts, is a similar waste. It's really like living in a dark room.

... Luang Por Chah taught us that our real task in life is to cultivate a healthy shame and fear of losing our mindfulness (*sati*). We must always strive to maintain *sati*. If we have *sati*, it's like we have an Ajahn with us. We feel warm and safe: whenever we make our mind steady, wisdom is ready to arise. Without *sati* we will always be slaves of our environment and simply follow whatever thoughts and moods arise.

Extracts from an 8 a.m. desanā *given by Luang Por Bundit*

Every second our thoughts and moods are teaching us. People without Right Understanding think, 'Why is it so hot?' or 'Why is it so cold?' But it's just nature doing its job. We don't have to make such a big deal out of it. If we don't understand the world, we will always experience *dukkha*. Disappointments will be difficult to accept and we'll always be living for our hopes and dreams.

... People used to come to pay respects to Luang Por Chah, and would complain they didn't have time to practise, that they were too busy looking after their children and everything else. 'Do you have time to breathe?' he would ask. 'Yes.' 'Well then, practise like that!'

Take up the five primary meditation objects that preceptors give the newly-ordained as a theme for contemplation: hair of the head, hair of the body, nails, teeth and skin. Doing this will help free us from being slaves to the body and all the usual concerns regarding beautification and health, and obsession with treatments and therapy.

Luang Por taught us to abandon everything. He repeated it again and again. In the old days there were no doubts about the correct practice, but now everyone has a different opinion about Luang Por's teachings.

So learn to choose the pure things in life. If you know those things which are pure and lead to peace, then you will bear witness to the truth yourself. No one can do it for you, or verify the fruit of your practice. It's *paccattaṃ* – to be experienced individually.

Well, that is enough for today, I'm sure everyone is very hungry. Learn to choose Dhamma teachings the way you choose the fish you eat. A fish has scales, bones, intestines, and flesh. Whether you choose the flesh is up to you.

This work is licensed under a Creative Commons
Attribution-NonCommercial-NoDerivs 3.0 Unported Licence.
http://creativecommons.org/licenses/by-nc-nd/3.0/

You are free:

- to copy, distribute, display and perform the work

Under the following conditions:

- Attribution: You must give the original author credit.
- Non-Commercial: You may not use this work for commercial purposes.
- No Derivative Works: You may not alter, transform, or build upon this work.

With the understanding that:

- Waiver: Any of the above conditions can be waived if you get permission from the copyright holder.
- Public Domain: Where the work or any of its elements is in the public domain under applicable law, that status is in no way affected by the licence.
- Other Rights: In no way are any of the following rights affected by the licence:
  - Your fair dealing or fair use rights, or other applicable copyright exceptions and limitations;
  - The author's moral rights;
  - Rights other persons may have either in the work itself or in how the work is used, such as publicity or privacy rights.
- Notice: For any reuse or distribution, you must make clear to others the licence terms of this work.

Amaravati Publications asserts its moral right to be identified as the author of this book.

Amaravati Publications requests that you attribute ownership of the work to Amaravati Publications on copying, distribution, display or performance of the work.

If you are interested in translating this text into another language, contact us for formatting guidelines, text material, and help with copyright issues on the addresses given at the front.